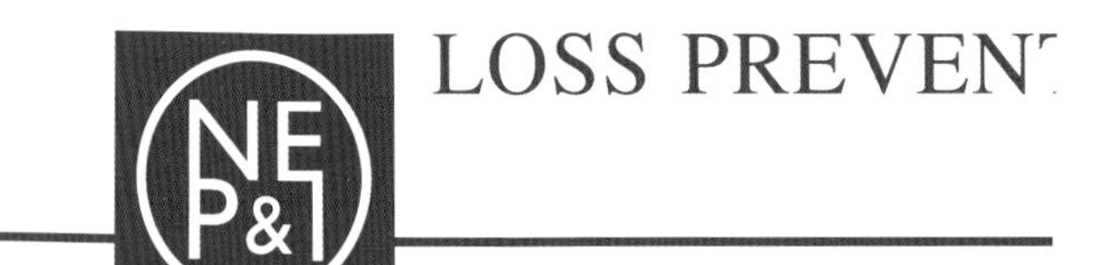

PERSONAL INJURY PREVENTION

A GUIDE TO GOOD PRACTICE

Second Edition

RICHARD BRACKEN IEng, AMIMarE

NORTH OF ENGLAND P&I ASSOCIATION

First edition published in 1996 by Roll Technical Marketing Limited
ISBN 0 9529820 0 5

Reprinted in 1998 by Anchorage Press
ISBN 0 9531785 1 X

Second edition published in 2003 by North of England P&I
Association Limited
The Quayside, Newcastle upon Tyne, NE1 3DU, United Kingdom

Telephone: +44 (0)191 232 5221
Fax: +44 (0)191 261 0540
Email: loss.prevention@nepia.com
Website: www.nepia.com

ISBN 0 9542012 7 2

Author: Richard Bracken, IEng, AMIMarE

Illustrator: Paul Windle

The publishers wish to thank the Controller of HMSO for permission to reproduce the hand signals illustration on page 40.

This guide is intended for general guidance only to assist in the prevention of personal injury, but it cannot apply to every situation and is to be used at the user's own risk. Readers should therefore take care to ensure that the recommendations contained in this guide are appropriate for any particular application before implementing them. No responsibility is accepted by the author, the North of England P&I Association Limited or by any firm, corporation or organisation who or which has been in any way concerned with the furnishing of information or data, the compilation, publication or authorised translation, supply or sale of this guide, for the accuracy of any information or advice given herein or for any omission here from or for any consequences whatsoever resulting directly or indirectly from compliance with or adoption of guidance contained herein.

CONTENTS

SAFETY NEEDS

YOU

CHAPTER 1

PERSONAL INJURY AND THE ROLE OF LOSS PREVENTION

In many shipping companies, shipboard safety has improved greatly over the past few years. With the implementation of the ISM Code, safety awareness programmes, the routine use of safety equipment, safety training and generally the development of a safety culture have made ships safer places to live and work. However, far too many incidents, accidents, injuries and claims are still occurring.

Clearly, such accidents lead to considerable suffering on the part of the individuals involved – and their families. They also lead to insurance claims which are a drain on the already overstretched ship owner's financial resources of shipowners

The apparent cause of personal injuries is frequently attributed to 'human error'. The true cause is often complex and involves many issues. It is the seafarers themselves, with guidance and support from the ship owner, safety advisers and legislation, who are best placed to investigate and analyse the causative factors which led to an accident. They can then implement corrective action in an effort to ensure that similar incidents do not happen again and generally assist in the reduction of personal injuries.

The word reduction is used since total elimination may not yet be a realistically viable target. But it is, nevertheless, what we should all strive for in the future.

It does not seem unreasonable to suggest that seafarers should take particular care for their own safety as well as that of their shipmates. Safety should be a priority consideration and tasks should only be attempted when all the safety implications have been fully considered and the appropriate action taken.

Many accidents are the result of lapses in concentration or have seemingly minor causes. The consequences of such lapses can lead to accidents which vary in their severity, but the degree of severity is often only down to chance.

Under the 'International Safety Management Code for the Safe Operation of Ships and Pollution Prevention', more commonly known as the International Safety Management (ISM) Code, all shipping companies are required to develop a safety and environmental policy as detailed in Section 1.4 of the Code – Functional requirements.

The Code, which is an International Maritime Organisation (IMO) resolution, has been incorporated as Chapter IX of the Safety of Life at Sea (SOLAS) Convention and is mandatory for almost all commercial ships around the world.

Section 7 of the Code requires the Company to establish procedures for the preparation of plans and instructions, including checklists as appropriate, for key shipboard operations concerning the safety of the ship. This sits alongside Section 8 which requires the Company to establish procedures to identify, describe and respond to emergency situations. This guide is not intended to fulfill those requirements in their entirety but provide a valuable complement to a ship owners own procedures. The manuals and procedures of each individual company Safety Management System must take precedence.

One of the listed objectives of the ISM Code is to:

'Provide for safe practices in ship operation and a safe working environment'.

This guide details a range of safe practices which, if adopted on board ship, will help reduce the high number of accidents and injuries experienced by many seafarers.

In essence, what must be developed is a safety culture.

Safety and accident prevention is really a four stage process. It is necessary to:

- Identify the size of the problem.
- Provide all personnel with basic training and basic personal protective equipment.
- Develop a safety culture – where safety becomes a priority consideration.
- Develop accident, incident and near miss reporting systems.

HOW BIG IS THE PROBLEM?

The deadline for compliance with phase 1 of the ISM Code was 1st July 1998. During the five years since 1998, the North of England P&I Club has been advised of over 19,000 claim incidents with an estimated value of over US $400 million. Of these, over 2,000 claims, with an estimated value of over US $50 million, were crew injury claims.

The pie charts on Page 3 show a percentage breakdown of claims by claim type both as the total number and cost of claims during the relevant period.

World-wide it is likely that crew injuries cost the shipping industry over US $175 million each year.

The problem is very serious and must demand everyone's attention.

BASIC SAFETY EQUIPMENT, TRAINING AND DEVELOPING THE SAFETY ETHOS

It is vital that all seafarers are provided with, and are trained in the proper use of, the correct safety equipment and personal protective equipment (PPE). This guide book attempts to identify that equipment and provide guidance on

VALUE OF CLAIMS—1998-2002

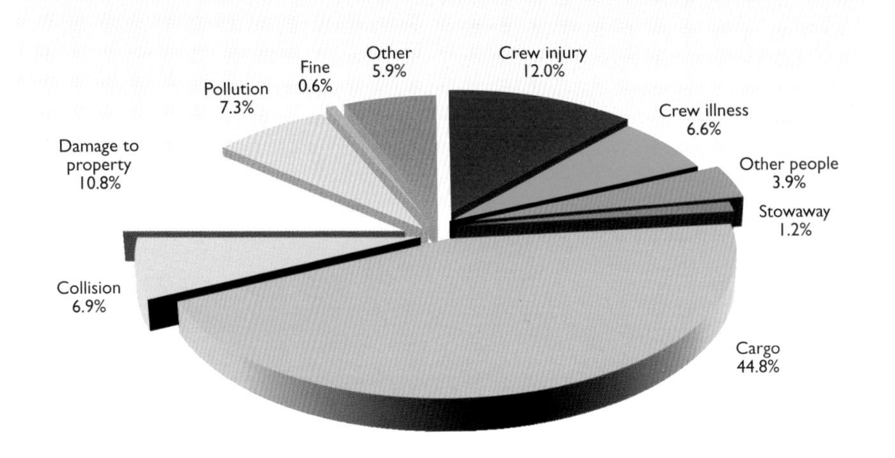

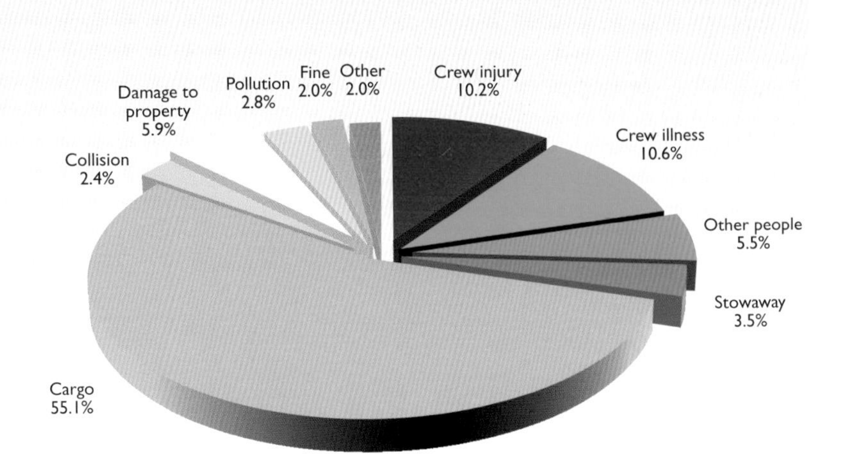

its use and the circumstances in which it should be used.

Once the equipment has been provided, and seafarers know how it should be correctly used, the next step is to develop the 'safety culture'. It is not enough to allow the management of safety to stop there – all involved must be motivated to put into practice what they have learned and to always use the correct PPE.

Developing the safety culture demands total commitment from the very top of the organisation, to drive it through the company managers, senior ship staff, officers and crew. This commitment must be a tangible one and safety and the prevention of personal injury must be elevated to become a priority factor in the operation of the company. It is vital to establish procedures, guidelines and advice to seafarers on practical means of avoiding personal injury.

The company role should be one of support and encouragement rather than one of developing more rules and regulations simply to comply with legislation. Encouragement, motivation and support of the sea staff by management will reap more benefits than increased regulation.

If they do not already do so, ship owners may wish to consider the appointment of a shore-based safety advisor who can visit ships providing advice on safety topics. During such visits he will be able to gain an impression of the safety awareness situation on board ship and the degree to which the safety culture has been developed. The opportunity may also be taken to provide safety training of sea staff within the context of the Safety Management System.

This guide is intended as an additional weapon in the fight against accidents – particularly personal injuries. It is not intended as an alternative to thorough training. The competency of seafarers to correctly use safety equipment and to be fully aware of on board safety procedures is of paramount importance. With the common goal of reducing the cost of personal injury in both human and financial terms, everyone has a responsibility and a role to play.

This obviously includes **you** – the reader!

CHAPTER 2

PERSONAL PROTECTIVE EQUIPMENT

Topics covered in this chapter

- Boilersuits
- Steel toe capped safety shoes
- Safety helmets
- Ear defenders – integral ear defenders
- Gloves
- Goggles and eye protection

Well-run companies already provide personal protective equipment to their sea staff. This chapter will identify a minimum standard, and the use of this equipment should be considered the norm. The items of personal protective equipment listed above should usually be provided to all personnel at the time of joining the ship.

These most basic items of personal safety equipment, and when they should be used, will now be briefly considered.

BOILERSUITS

Boilersuits, or 'cover-alls' as they are called in some parts of the world, should be worn at all times outside the living areas of the accommodation, except the wheelhouse, as they provide all over body protection. They are made of high quality durable materials and afford protection from oils, greases, dirt and other potential hazards found on board ship. They also, in their simplest role, keep other items of clothing clean.

Boilersuits should be worn fastened up at the neck and wrist and be kept in good condition. Torn, damaged or oil impregnated boilersuits should be washed and repaired. If repair is not possible, then they should be disposed of and new ones issued.

Some companies allocate different coloured boilersuits to personnel from different departments on board ship, claiming this aids identification and may make personnel more visible in particular working environments.

SAFETY SHOES

Safety shoes should be worn at all times when working outside the accommodation. This includes galleys, stores and refrigeration spaces. They should also be worn when carrying out maintenance or repairs in the accommodation. There is, of course, an argument that working boots will dirty accommodation carpets, and so on. To avoid this, persons likely to be working in the accommodation should be issued with 'clean' working boots (an additional pair of boots) or plastic boot covers. However, care must be taken to avoid the risk of slipping on polished floors, for example, when wearing such boot protectors.

Safety shoes also provide protection from slips and falls as well as protection from crush and impact injuries. Safety shoes should be resistant to chemicals, acids and oils.

NB: When Wellington boots are used in the workplace, for example washing down and similar jobs, then steel toe capped Wellingtons should be worn.

Suitable footwear should be worn at all times, including off duty periods and the use of backless slippers, flip-flops and the like should be avoided wherever possible.

SAFETY HELMETS

Safety helmets provide personal protection from impact damage, bumps and knocks as well as from falling objects. The wearing of safety helmets by all personnel should be encouraged at all times when outside of the accommodation area.

As a minimum, however, they should be worn during the following on board activities.

- All mooring, unmooring, tug handling and anchoring operations.
- All emergency stations – boat drills, fire drills, rescue drills and helicopter operation drills.
- Storing operations.
- All lifting operations.
- Cargo work and bunkering operations.
- All engine room maintenance.
- At anytime outside the accommodation whilst in port or in refit / dry dock.

The wearing of safety helmets will help to prevent head injuries, facial injury and brain damage. Ideally they should be fitted and worn with integral / helmet mounted ear defenders and chin straps.

Some seafarers will argue that safety helmets are intrusive and are not viable due to the high temperatures encountered on board ship. Helmets are now relatively lightweight, they may have shortened peaks to enable easier vision and may have ventilation holes. They are not difficult to wear, but it may take some time before the wearer becomes fully at ease with them. Once again, some companies allocate different coloured hats to shipboard personnel for emergency parties, for instance fire parties and emergency response teams.

Safety helmets usually have a service life or date of manufacture embossed on them. Helmets should be replaced when out of date. Helmets should not be painted, written on or have stickers stuck on them. They must be maintained in good condition and replaced if they suffer a heavy blow or impact.

EAR DEFENDERS – INTEGRAL EAR DEFENDERS

Ear defenders and / or integral ear defenders can provide ship's staff with protection from the loud and noisy environments to which they may be exposed during every working day. Hearing loss is directly related to such exposure and can be permanent. The industry is still seeing frequent claims for industrial deafness although the cause has been known, and the personal protective equipment has been available, for many years. It is difficult to say what noise level causes specific degrees of hearing loss. However, it is probably true to say that if conversation is difficult then the environment is likely to cause permanent damage. In these circumstances it is recommended that ear defenders are worn. They should always be worn in the following spaces

- engine rooms
- hydraulic rooms
- crane machinery spaces
- fan rooms
- pump rooms
- refrigeration compressor spaces
- cargo pump rooms.

Ear defenders should be maintained in good order and replaced or reconditioned using approved hygiene kits if their serviceability is in doubt.

GLOVES

Gloves should be worn whenever their use will help prevent injury. The type of gloves used depends on the tasks being undertaken. Leather palm general duty gloves should be worn during most general duties although it is appreciated that they can be difficult if handling small components. Other types of gloves should be used where appropriate, for example

- chemical resistant rubber gloves when handling acids, alkalies and shipboard chemicals
- leather or heat resistant gauntlets when conducting hot work

- rubber gloves when handling household cleaning agents
- insulated rubber gloves for electrical work.

These are a few examples of the different types of gloves available. Each situation should be considered on its merits and only gloves approved for the purpose should be used. However the message is clear – use gloves whenever possible and if in doubt seek further advice.

General duty gloves should be kept clean and oil free wherever possible so as to avoid loss of grip when climbing ladders, etc. If gloves do become oil impregnated they should be replaced. Gloves used for chemicals and petroleum products should be rinsed with fresh water after use.

As with all safety equipment, gloves must be kept in good order or replaced.

GOGGLES AND EYE PROTECTION

Goggles and eye protection should be worn when or wherever there is a risk of eye injury. They should always be worn when

- operating machine tools
- handling shipboard chemicals
- using cleaning agents
- using welding or burning equipment
- using pressure washing equipment
- anchoring
- operating shot-blasting equipment, needle guns or chipping hammers
- using grinding equipment
- there is any risk of an eye injury.

Several types of eye protection are available, including visors, box type goggles and safety spectacles. Each have their merits, but it is suggested box type goggles offer the best general service. They offer full eye protection and can be worn over conventional glasses. This type of goggle can suffer from condensation problems in high ambient temperatures, but this problem may be overcome by purchasing goggles with suitable ventilation provision. The protection used will be directly dependent on the duties that are to be attempted. Visors offer full facial protection but incidents have occurred where chemicals, particles etc have caused injury by getting under or behind such visors. As always exercise caution and choose protective equipment with care and with due regard to the task being undertaken.

Only goggles approved for their intended use should be worn. If in doubt clarify the correct type to be used. Do not use non-classified goggles, safety goggles usually have approval marks of protection codes clearly marked on them.

ADDITIONAL PERSONAL PROTECTIVE EQUIPMENT

This includes the following items.

- Safety harnesses.
- Safety belts.
- Buoyancy aids.
- Welding goggles and visors.
- Welding gauntlets, aprons and gaiters.
- Thermal jackets.
- Dust masks.
- Life lines.
- Portable radios.
- Portable – individual gas detection alarms.
- Chemical suits.
- Fire suits.
- Respirators with correct filter inserts.
- Reflective jackets.

It must be remembered that each task must be evaluated, at the work planning meeting, on its own merit and the correct levels of personal protective equipment established before the job is started. All equipment should be checked, inspected and tested in accordance with manufacturer's instructions and ship owner's instructions.

This list of personal protective equipment is far from exhaustive but should provide a minimum checklist to be considered when assessing the job in hand at the work planning stage.

CHAPTER 3

SHIPBOARD SAFETY MANAGEMENT

Topics covered in this chapter

- Management meetings
- Shipboard safety committee
- Shipboard safety officer
- Safety tours for new joiners
- Safety representatives
- Daily work planning meetings
- Weekly work planning meetings

Safety is of paramount importance and should be borne in mind before any task is attempted. In order to get this message across, it is necessary to develop a safety culture where all staff appreciate the importance of safety. In fact, it must be their first consideration and become part of their way of life.

The senior officers on the ship, in particular, must be totally committed to the safety culture and must be seen to actively promote and support its development. Everyone onboard should actively promote safety.

To assist in the management of safety onboard ship, working parties or committees should be set up. Indeed, the promotion of teamwork is an important part of any good onboard safety management system.

MANAGEMENT MEETING

The senior officers, collectively known as the management team, should meet on a regular basis, normally weekly, to discuss all aspects relating to the safe operation and running of the vessel. However, safety should be high on the agenda.

The safety officer should report the outcome of the safety committee meeting to the management meeting and if there are any points outstanding from the safety meeting these should be addressed by the management team. If shipboard procedures need to be amended or operational directives need to be reviewed the management meeting would be the correct forum to investigate the necessary changes.

Someone in the ship owner's office should be identified to accept safety enquiries and a direct route to this person should be established – the Designated

ENGINE ROOM
No smoking

ENGINE R
USE S FE
EQUI M NT

Person (DP) required under Section 4 of the ISM Code may be an obvious choice. As a rule, this person should nurture a good relationship with the ship, always respond to safety queries and attend shipboard meetings, if at all possible, as this will show active support of the sea staff.

SHIPBOARD SAFETY COMMITTEE

A safety committee should be the onboard focal point for the ship's safety effort. The members of the safety committee should normally include

- master
- shipboard safety officer
- officers' representative
- crew representative
- committee secretary.

The officers and crew representatives should be elected by fellow officers and crew as should the secretary. However, it is useful to bear in mind that one volunteer is better than ten pressed men.

If the safety committee is 'top heavy' with senior staff then the free flow of information can be stifled. It is this free flow of information that is so vital if a safety culture is to be developed. It is the main forum, although not the only one, where safety matters can be raised. Ship's staff should not delay reporting safety matters until the next safety meeting but should be free to discuss their concerns as and when necessary. Everyone should be encouraged to contribute and the safety committee should report to the management committee. Minutes should be kept of all safety meetings and these minutes sent to appropriate shore-based personnel who should respond and at the very least acknowledge safe receipt.

THE SHIPBOARD SAFETY OFFICER

The shipboard safety officer should be nominated by the company and may typically be one of the more experienced junior officers. On ships sailing with traditional manning arrangements this would typically be the second officer or third engineer. Some companies have nominated senior officers, i.e. chief officer, chief or second engineers as shipboard safety officers.

The thinking behind this is sound, in as much as these are experienced officers with in depth knowledge of shipboard operations and are often better able to enforce safety guidelines and regulations. However, problems may arise if a conflict of interest situation occurs.

If a job or task needs to be completed quickly, it could be that a second engineer who is also serving as the safety officer will feel obliged to sanction short cuts to the detriment of his safety concerns. This may not be a conscious decision but due to perceived or real pressures. A safety officer with no direct responsibility for maintenance or workloads may be better able to consider the safety aspects more objectively.

Whoever is nominated, this role as safety officer should be part of their job description and the officer should be allocated time for these duties. The safety officer should, with the full co-operation of the ship's complement, co-ordinate the safety effort. He will have access to the ship's safety library, will be in a position to advise on safety matters and should attend work planning meetings. To assist him to carry out these duties the appointed officer should have attended a suitable training course wherever possible.

The shipboard safety officer should initiate and co-ordinate safety tours for all new joiners. A tour around the vessel should point out the location of safety equipment and give advice on its use. All potential hazards should be highlighted. During this safety tour the location of muster stations, emergency stations, alarm points, fire fighting equipment and breathing apparatus should be identified. This safety tour should be carried out as soon after personnel join the vessel as possible. Indeed, visitors and supernumeraries should also be given such a tour, amended as necessary, to suit their individual requirements.

An inspection programme should be established and the shipboard safety officer should conduct regular tours of the vessel to ensure safety is getting the attention it deserves.

SAFETY REPRESENTATIVES

Depending on the size of ship and its crew, safety representatives from the shipboard departments should be elected to sit on the safety committee. The representatives should feel free and be encouraged to voice their concerns as well as those of the people they represent. Wherever possible they should support the safety officer particularly when considering safety aspects outside of the safety officers professional field, for example when the safety officer is a deck officer and a representative may be from the catering department.

DAILY WORK PLANNING MEETINGS

Daily work planning meetings are essential if work is to be professionally planned, safety aspects fully considered and inter-departmental effects discussed. The chief engineer, chief officer, second engineer, safety officer and senior rating should attend work meetings wherever possible and the master may also wish to attend.

The meetings should be carried out in the true spirit of the safety culture, rather than just be an opportunity for a chat. The jobs for the next day should be itemised and the safety aspects identified. Work permits, hot work permits, and so on, should be arranged if they are necessary.

Minutes should be produced, detailing jobs, responsibilities and safety, as discussed at the meeting and these minutes should be distributed to the ship's complement. This will be the daily work plan.

No jobs should be attempted unless they have been fully discussed and detailed on the daily work plan. If something unexpected occurs onboard then all safety aspects should be discussed and an unscheduled work permit completed. This should be signed by a senior officer or the job supervisor.

On vessels with small crews, meetings need not be formal but all relevant personnel should endeavour to get together to discuss plans for the next day. Such a meeting may be held in the wheel house but topics including proposed work, job allocation and interdepartmental effects must be discussed.

WEEKLY WORK MEETINGS

Weekly work meetings should be arranged to plan the major jobs ahead particularly to consider equipment requirements, inter-departmental effects and safety aspects.

The opportunity should be taken at the meeting to consider whether it is necessary to order spares, obtain specialist safety equipment or simply to ensure that the actions of one department will not adversely affect another.

This meeting is another shipboard forum to promote good communication, teamwork and safety.

As with all management situations, the establishment of good relationships is vital. If things go well, praise the staff. Encourage the free flow of information and, most importantly, act on information received.

Safety is all about good communication, work planning, preparation and relationships.

SAFETY
YOU

RoCK

CHAPTER 4

WORK PLANNING AND PROCEDURES

Topics covered in this chapter

- Job allocation
- Equipment requirements
- Inter-departmental effects
- Daily work plans
- Detailed job procedures
- Permit to work systems
- Example of a permit to work situation

Many near misses, accidents and injuries occur because tasks were badly planned or poor procedures were adopted.

The setting up of formal work planning meetings, as detailed in the Shipboard Safety Management Section, will greatly assist the safety effort and will provide a forum to establish correct safety procedures.

At the work planning meeting all of the safety aspects relating to a task should be considered. Particular factors which must be considered should include job allocation, equipment requirements, levels of personal training, and inter-departmental effects. Specific safety equipment requirements and personal safety equipment should also be identified. The necessary safety equipment must then be made available and checked prior to the commencement of any tasks.

When major jobs are to be attempted it is often prudent to prepare a detailed work plan for a specific task which can be distributed with the daily work plan. Such detailed plans can play an important role in allowing all participants to have an overview of the task, and can be very specific. Occasions warranting such detailed plans may include

- major engine maintenance
- entry into bunker tanks
- major boiler cleans
- tank washing / cleaning
- work in enclosed spaces

- tank or void space inspections
- cargo operations.

When the work plan is formulated and established, the way in which tasks are to be approached and completed should also be discussed. Established procedures enable everyone to be made aware of how the task is to be tackled and which safety aspects are important.

Many routine tasks carried out on board are potentially dangerous and the slightest deviation from an established routine may lead to an accident or serious injury. It should also be appreciated that some established routines are not always the safest and consideration should always be given to how to introduce improved practices and safer methods.

One method which may be employed to avoid such incidents is the 'permit to work' system. This system has proved a very effective loss prevention tool and should be adopted on all vessels. Under this system no task should be started without a valid permit. Typical examples include the following.

- Hot work.
- Electrical work.
- Machinery maintenance.
- Entry into enclosed spaces.
- Working aloft / overside.

Work should not begin until any machinery and electrical equipment has been fully isolated and 'danger notices' posted. These notices are to be in a prominent position to alert others to the potential dangers.

It is essential that the importance of such permits is fully appreciated and any person signing a permit should personally check all aspects of the permit. A completed permit should be signed by the head of department.

During periods of high workload, the implementation of the 'permit to work' system may be difficult, but lives could be endangered if it is not followed properly. If a person has been asked to sign a permit but is unable to check out all the safety aspects or implications they should not sign. The job should not be allowed to proceed.

Permits should cover only those tasks detailed in the permit and the permit should only be valid for specified periods of time.

FOR EXAMPLE

If a group of sailors are mopping and cleaning in the pump room of a product tanker then a valid permit should have been issued before entry into the pump room is allowed. The permit should only be valid for the period of time specified by the signatory. If at any time prevailing conditions change, problems arise or the time period elapses all personnel must vacate the pump room. The atmosphere should be re-tested and proven safe prior to the issue of another entry permit. Then, and only then, should personnel be permitted to re-enter the pump room.

Permits to work do not, in themselves, stop accidents but they will encourage the adoption of a system which will convey the information clearly, unambiguously and avoid many of the misinterpretations encountered when purely verbal methods are used. They also define specific procedures prior to the commencement of work and it is this that helps prevent accidents.

Other procedures include the use of checklists which are becoming more popular and should be encouraged in both deck and engine departments. They can prove particularly useful during officer handovers and prior to duties which are carried out on a routine basis when simple errors are often made due to over familiarity. An example would be a pre-unmanned machinery space checklist, detailing all aspects for consideration prior to allowing an engine room to become unmanned.

REPLACE ALL TOOLS AFTER USE
EMERGENCY STOPS
STOP

CHAPTER 5

WORKSHOP PRACTICES – USING MACHINE AND HAND TOOLS

Topics covered in this chapter

- Machine tools
- Hand tools
- Power tools
- Tool guards
- Workshop tidiness

Unfortunately, far too many accidents still occur in workshops, machinery spaces and on deck when using machine tools and hand tools. Many such injuries could be avoided by adopting safe practices.

There is a correct tool for every job and any tool being used for a purpose for which it is not designed is a potential hazard. All staff should be trained in the use of both hand and machine tools prior to using them. All tools should be maintained in good working order, only being used for the duties for which they are designed. Operating guides and manuals should be circulated and readily available. All tools should be stowed carefully and on completion of the task in hand they should be returned to the correct storage location, cleaned and prepared for future use.

Damaged, worn or potentially hazardous tools must not be used and should be taken out of service. When this course of action is taken the relevant head of department should be advised. The tools should only be returned to service when all faults are rectified. If it proves impossible to repair a tool, it should be disposed of or destroyed.

Some faults may be simple to rectify, but if they remain unrepaired they will lead to injuries. Such fault rectification may include dressing chisels, sharpening punches or fitting a new file handle.

Hand held power tools can be potentially very dangerous and should only be used in accordance with manufacturers' instructions and operated by experienced and trained staff. Such tools may be driven by electricity, battery or compressed air, but the same fundamental safety rules apply in each case.

All plugs, cables, fittings and connections should be regularly checked and any fuses fitted should be of minimum serviceable rating. For work carried out in confined spaces, tools should be of the low voltage type – typically 24V. If low voltage supplies and tools are not readily available on board vessels, then ship owners must consider the possibility of purchasing portable transformer units and low voltage hand tools. Any equipment used in hazardous areas should be intrinsically safe and maintained correctly. Such intrinsically safe equipment should be labeled with the correct approvals.

Operating triggers on hand held power tools should never be 'fixed' either by using wire or jubilee clips. This is a very dangerous practice.

No maintenance should be attempted on any power tool before it has been isolated from its power source. Even basic operations such as changing drill bits should only be attempted when the drill has been isolated.

The improper use of workshop machine tools results in many accidents and injuries and such machine tools should only ever be operated by trained and competent personnel. In this section all secured machine tools are included except welding machines which will be considered separately.

The first and most important thing any machine tool operator must know is how to stop the machine. Various methods may be employed, including stop buttons, emergency stop kick bars and emergency stops, to name but a few, but the single most important lesson is this.

Never start a machine unless you know how to stop it !

All stopping methods should be clearly indicated. Emergency remote 'stops' capable of stopping all workshop machines should be sited around the workshop.

Guards should be fitted to all machine tools and no machine should be operated unless guards are in place. Guards should only be of approved designs and must be fully compatible with the machine.

Even with guards fitted, the operator should always wear approved goggles whenever there is a risk of eye injury.

Artificial lighting in workshops should be carefully selected to avoid the potential stroboscopic effect of fluorescent lights on rotating machinery.

As with power tools, if a machine is considered defective it should be taken out of service, until it is repaired and tested. In the meantime it should be isolated and 'danger notices' posted.

Some machines, pedestal grinding machines for example, may be belt driven and consequently these belts should be well maintained with belt guards fitted. These guards should only be removed when the machine is confirmed fully isolated.

Simple things such as swarf removal, chuck keys left in chucks, unguarded machines and unsecured work pieces still lead to too many accidents and injuries. Clothing should be fastened and hair should be secured or tied up so as to prevent entanglement in rotating machinery.

All workshops should be kept clean and tidy with all tools returned to shadow boards, which allow easy identification of missing tools. The workshop should be uncluttered and all benches, decks and machines should be tidied between jobs and each evening.

Areas in the immediate vicinity of machines can be enclosed by grid lines painted on the deck within which nothing should be placed or stored.

All machines should be cleaned and swept down after use. However, the use of compressed air for this purpose can be very dangerous and must be prohibited.

✔

✘

CHAPTER 6

GOOD HOUSEKEEPING

Topics covered in this chapter

- Good housekeeping
- Unmanned machinery spaces
- Reporting deficiencies
- Securing equipment, stores and belongings
- Garbage

Good housekeeping is a vital part of shipboard safety management and is an area worthy of great attention. Personal injury statistics indicate that 45% of all injuries are as a result of slips and falls.

Good housekeeping must be actively encouraged and senior officers must promote it.

All personnel should always ensure that they

- keep the work place clean, tidy and well lit
- always clear up oil spills, however small
- remove obstacles
- clearly mark and effectively fence off openings in decks or gratings
- clearly mark safe paths of access for visitors and crew
- return tools after use
- promptly dispose of garbage and waste in accordance with legislation
- rectify oil leaks before they become too serious – buckets or catch pots should not be used
- keep all equipment and stores properly secured.

The chief officer or his representative should complete evening rounds in a thorough and seamanlike manner and ensure the deck is safe and secure before nightfall.

The watchkeeping engineer should ensure that all machinery spaces are clean and tidy during his watch and that all potential hazards are dealt with as soon as they become apparent. On vessels operating unmanned machinery spaces (UMS), the duty engineer should ensure that the engine room is left in a safe condition. It might prove advantageous for the senior engineers to develop a pre UMS checklist that must be completed prior to the engine room going unmanned. The list might include checking that all fire alarms are reinstated and that the officer of the watch on the bridge is advised that the engine room is about to go UMS.

Generally all deficiencies should be rectified as soon as possible – a delay may lead to an accident and the possible injury of a shipmate. Faulty lighting, damaged handrails and obstructed stairs may all seem innocuous, but left unattended they are very real hazards. In addition, save-alls should be kept clean and oil free. Buckets or drums of petroleum products used for cleaning, and typically found being used for cleaning purifiers and fuel components, should be emptied after use and prior to going UMS.

Running lights should be operational, and machinery instructions and notices should be legible, as well as clear and concise. All machinery operating instructions should be prepared in the language of the operators. If machinery or pipe-work lagging is damaged then it should be correctly repaired. If asbestos lagging has been used on a ship then it should be brought to the owner's attention and dealt with by professionals.

As all seafarers are aware, vessels are seldom still, but in times of rough weather all items on board, from cabin ornaments to main engine spares, should be correctly secured.

Garbage deserves special mention particularly in light of current legislation. Waste should be sorted prior to disposal into plastics, bio-degradable waste and galley waste. However, some items, including aerosols and batteries, should always be segregated and never incinerated on board, but should be retained for disposal ashore. An exploding aerosol can is a significant hazard and may seriously injure a friend or colleague. All waste bins, particularly those containing oily rags, cotton waste or machining swarf and that constitute a potential fire hazard should be emptied prior to vacating the engine room.

Much of this is common sense. Yet all too often injuries and claims arise as a result of these types of mistakes.

How many times have doors been left neither secured open nor shut, but swinging? Yet it is well known that ships roll. How many times have gratings or floor plates been removed and left unguarded, or oil spills left and not cleared up? It is particularly important that all emergency escape routes are kept clear and well lit. Escape hatches should be clearly marked to ensure nothing is placed on hatch lids. This is vital to ensure that escape is possible at all times.

To sum up, good housekeeping is essential. Without it, accidents, injuries and claims will always happen.

CHAPTER 7

ELECTRICAL MAINTENANCE

Topics covered in this chapter

- Potential risks
- Ambient conditions
- Electrical equipment isolation procedures
- Responding to electric shock
- Storage batteries
- Personal electrical equipment

The potential risks associated with electricity and work on electrical equipment are well known, but still far too many electrical related accidents occur leading to seafarers being injured. Prevailing conditions on board ship often create increased risks of electric shock due to the wet, damp, humid conditions so often encountered on ships. High ambient temperatures cause sweating, thus reducing body resistance, as do skin abrasions and cuts. In such difficult working conditions, severe, even fatal, electric shocks can be caused by voltages as low as 60V. When one considers that some vessels have power supplies of 11kV, it is obvious that work on such plant is potentially very hazardous.

The message is: proceed with extreme caution.

Before any maintenance of any electrical equipment is attempted the job should be discussed at the work planning meeting and all the safety aspects given due consideration.

Personnel involved in electrical maintenance should be familiar with test procedures, isolation techniques and equipment requirements. In no circumstances should work commence before the power supply has been isolated and a permit to work system adopted. (The permit to work system is discussed in Chapter 4).

With the power supply isolated, all fuses, switches and / or circuit breakers should be isolated / removed and locked. Those persons conducting maintenance which involves removing fuses should whenever possible keep these fuses with them. 'Danger notices' should be posted at all positions where power could be reconnected. Even then, no work should be attempted before checking isolation with a multimeter. Then, and only then, should work begin on the electrical equipment.

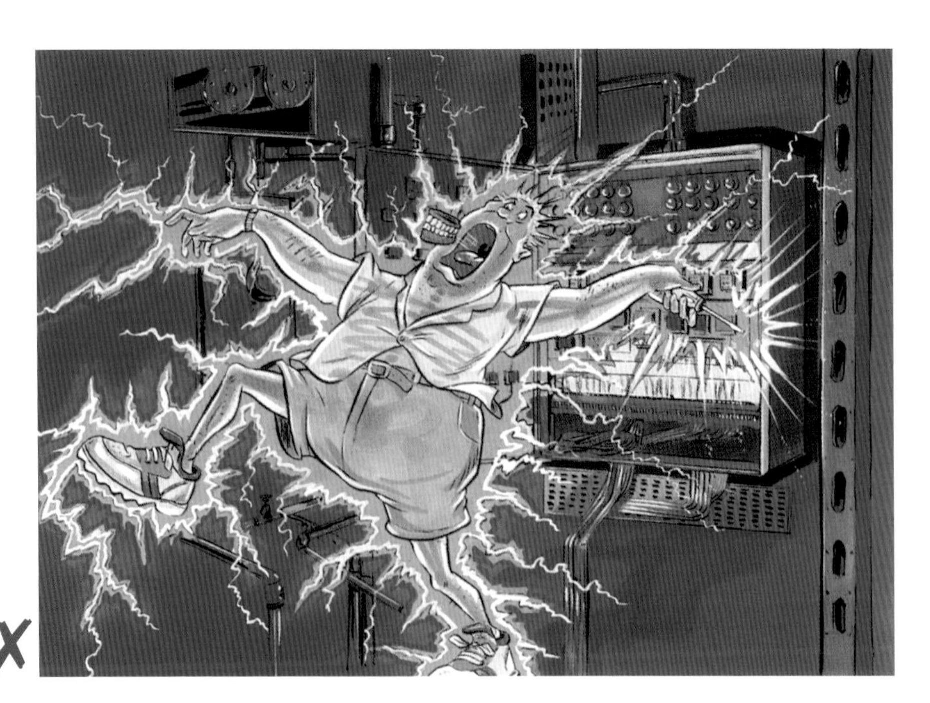

No person should work alone on electrical equipment. A second man should always be in attendance, and he should be aware of emergency procedures and what to do if anything goes wrong. He should also be familiar with the treatment of electric shock victims and remain at the job location until work is complete. He should not, however, stand behind the man carrying out the maintenance, as in the event of electric shock the men could collide.

In the event of electric shock the stand-by man should isolate the power supply and then remove the casualty from the power source. In the situation where low voltage equipment is involved, and it is not possible to isolate the supply, it may be possible to remove the person from the source using a piece of wood or a similar non conductive material. Avoid bodily contact whilst the casualty is still touching the power source.

Seek assistance as soon as possible by raising the alarm.

Precautionary safety equipment should be used. This includes dry, insulating mats, insulated gloves and insulated tools.

Equipment with poor insulating qualities should be avoided, as should damp humid environments wherever possible, and as much of the body as possible should be covered. Metal to metal contact should be avoided as should the wearing of metal jewellery and watches.

On vessels operating with Unmanned Machinery Spaces (UMS), if a duty engineer is called to the engine room with an electrical problem, he should ask for assistance even if only trying to locate an earth fault.

If switchboard panels are removed for maintenance, they should be immediately replaced on completion of the job in hand and during the intervening period they should be fenced / roped off areas.

STORAGE BATTERIES

Storage batteries have been included in this section as they are part of vessel's electrical outfit but often are not treated with the respect they deserve.

Any type of storage battery should be well maintained and kept in a designated battery locker. This locker should be fitted with sufficient means of ventilation since hydrogen gas, given off by storage batteries being charged, is easily ignited and could cause a serious explosion. With this in mind, smoking should be prohibited in the battery locker and the use of equipment capable of generating sources of ignition also prohibited. Fixed lighting arrangements should be intrinsically safe, to the recommended standard and correctly maintained.

Battery terminal connections should be maintained tight and greased with batteries securely clamped. Storage batteries are often heavy and for this reason, as well as to avoid spilling electrolyte, they should be carried with extreme care and additional manpower used as necessary.

When working with batteries, goggles, chemical rubber gloves and protective suits or aprons should be worn. Men working on storage batteries should be aided by a second man as above. Eye wash bottles should be kept in the battery locker but these MUST be easily distinguished from any other containers in the locker.

Wherever possible lead acid and alkaline batteries should be stored in separate lockers. If this is not possible then they should be separated by a screen. All types of batteries should be maintained in accordance with manufacturers instructions. Tools used for maintaining lead acid batteries should not be used for alkaline batteries.

All shipboard electrical equipment should be inspected and approved for use on board ship. This even includes personal electrical appliances such as stereos, televisions and computers.

CHAPTER 8

HANDLING SHIPBOARD CHEMICALS

Topics covered in this chapter

- Sources of information for shipboard chemicals
- Control of shipboard chemicals
- Handling chemicals
- Pollution incidents and fires involving chemicals

All personnel involved in the handling, stowage, storage and use of shipboard chemicals should be familiar and fully conversant with the potential hazards. They must also be familiar with emergency procedures and what to do in the event of a spillage.

Manufacturers' advice notices, data sheets, and other relevant information, should be prominently displayed and anyone coming into contact with such chemicals should read this information.

Ideally all shipboard chemicals should be stored in a central store, a dedicated chemical locker, protected with fire detection and extinguishing systems. Outside the chemical lockers, dedicated showers should be fitted with easy to operate quick release flow control valves. Protective clothing should be stored directly outside the chemical locker including: chemical suits, Wellington boots, gloves or gauntlets, goggles and eye wash bottles. Where non-compatible chemicals are stored onboard these should be distinctly separated. This may be within the main chemical locker but it may be necessary to use a separate designated storage area.

Data sheets and / manufacturers safety notices should be placed inside and outside the chemical locker. Danger warning notices should clearly identify chemicals.

Access to chemicals should be restricted and only allowed under controlled procedures. Chemical lockers should be locked and keys held by appropriate personnel.

If ready use chemicals are required the chemical required should be withdrawn from the chemical locker and taken to the location required. Here, it should only be used by personnel wearing suitable personal protective equipment, then unused chemical returned to the chemical locker. A record of the contents of all drums and the chemical locker should be kept and all records updated when any withdrawals or stocktaking takes place.

RESTRICTED ACCESS KEEP LOCKED
DATA SHEETS

The indiscriminate storage of chemicals around the vessel should be avoided wherever possible. If this is unavoidable, for example in chemical testing and treatment bays, these areas should be provided with the full range of protective equipment required for the chemical in use.

It must be appreciated that all chemicals are a potential hazard; from the everyday detergents to the very strong boiler treatment chemicals found on some vessels such as 'hydrazine'. It is recommended that all chemicals are stored in the centralised chemical store and only withdrawn, in a controlled manner, as required. The indiscriminate mixing of chemicals must be avoided and any mixing should only be allowed when approved by manufacturers. Indeed all substances including household goods should be handled with care and not mixed indiscriminately.

All chemicals must be handled with extreme care and only when personal protective equipment is employed. Chemicals should only be used where the contents of containers is beyond doubt.

In the event of a spillage, this should be cleaned up promptly but with due regard to safety and pollution regulations. If there is likely to be a build up of gases or vapours, the space should be evacuated and re-entry only considered when the area is proven safe or with breathing apparatus.

In the event of any fire involving chemicals, due consideration should be given to the particular chemicals involved when attempting to extinguish it.

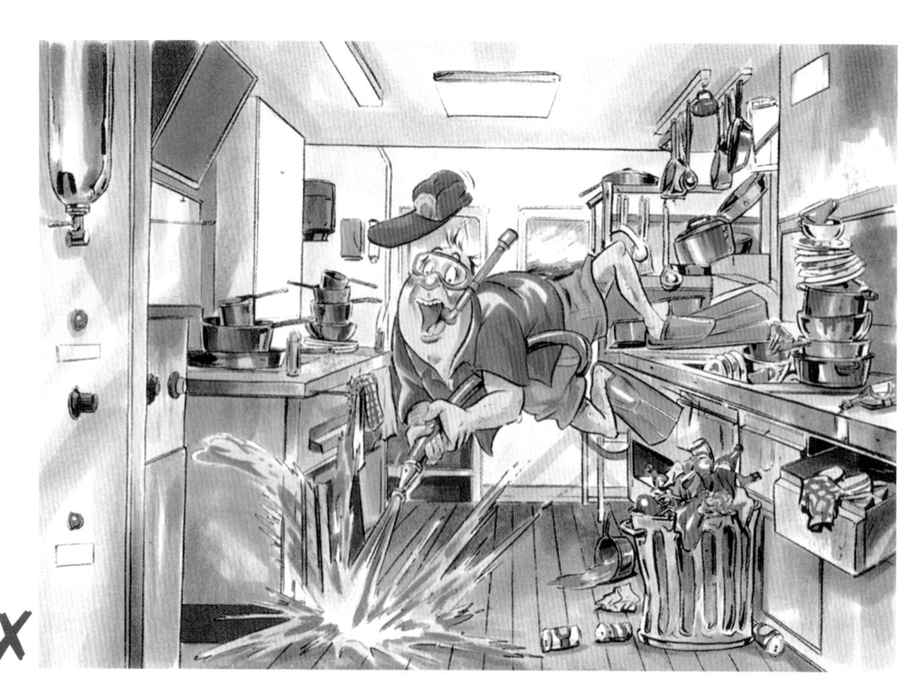

CHAPTER 9

GALLEYS – CATERING AND PERSONAL HYGIENE

Topics covered in this chapter

- Personal hygiene
- Injuries involving sharp objects
- Galley cleanliness
- Galley slips and falls
- Refrigerated spaces
- Isolating galley equipment

All ship's personnel should take particular care when cleaning themselves to prevent dermatitis and other skin infections. The use of specialist hand cleaners should be actively encouraged. This is particularly the case with catering staff working in galleys, mess rooms, saloons and pantries.

Hands and finger nails must be cleaned prior to the handling or preparation of food stuffs. This is especially important after visiting toilets, handling galley waste, garbage, cleaning and handling uncooked foods. All catering staff should wear the correct personal safety equipment and such equipment and clothing should be maintained in a clean, tidy condition. Utensil cleanliness is imperative. Cracked or damaged china wear should be destroyed.

Many accidents occur as a result of submerged knives and glasses (sharps) in galley and pantry washing up bowls and sinks. All 'sharps' should be left in a dry bowl or by the sink and only submerged by the person designated to do the washing up. Personnel should take care to ensure that sharps left by sinks and bowls cannot accidentally fall into the same bowls and sinks. Care should also be taken whilst using cleaning substances and the use of protective gloves or dishwashers is recommended.

The general cleanliness of the galley spaces is imperative and these spaces should be cleaned daily – usually at the end of each working day. Particular care should be taken when washing down as the indiscriminate use of hoses, buckets, and so on, can be very dangerous. Many electrical earths on board ship are sourced in galleys during washing down. Areas of particular note include: galley ranges, sinks, galley decks and ventilation grids. The grids often fitted above the galley range become clogged with grease and dirt. Galley bins, slops and waste food should be collected, sorted and disposed of in compliance with current international and regional legislation.

A large number of injuries in galley and catering spaces are the result of slips and falls. Particular attention should be paid to the avoidance of such injuries.

Personnel working in the catering areas should wear anti-slip, steel toe capped, boots and never flip – flops, sandals, training shoes, etc. All spills must be cleared up immediately.

Another area in which many injuries occur is refrigerated spaces. These spaces should be well lit, fitted with duck boards on the deck and personnel alarms. Doors should be secured open during storing and the in-room door release mechanisms tested regularly. Refrigerant leakage detectors should be fitted or personnel entering refrigerated spaces should be issued with portable detectors. Items stored in fridge spaces should be secured to avoid injury in heavy weather – frozen meat, for example, can be very heavy. Persons entering refrigerated spaces should wear suitable thermal clothing including gloves, hats and thermal suits to prevent frost bite and exposure to extreme cold and they should advise a responsible officer prior to entering a refrigerated space.

In the galley itself there is always a serious risk of burns, scalds, and other injuries, and this is a problem that can be exacerbated when the vessel is moving in a seaway. Range bars, or fiddles as they are often known, should be fitted on galley ranges to avoid pots and pans sliding across the range. Pans should only be filled to safe levels. Extreme care should be taken when removing large dishes and similar heavy items from hot ovens. Deep fat fryers are a particular source of potential injury and should be treated with caution, maintained in good working order, and kept clean and tidy.

All galley equipment, galley ranges, bakers ovens, deep fat fryers, toasters and similar appliances should all be isolated at the end of each working day.

High standards of personal hygiene should be maintained by all ship's staff and all clothing should be regularly washed. The use of oil soaked boilersuits and similar working clothes should be avoided. When washing clothing ensure all soap is washed out and thoroughly rinsed. Infections / diseases such as ringworm, dermatitis and 'dhobi rash' can result if this simple step is not taken.

CHAPTER 10

LIFTING AND LIFTING APPLIANCES

Topics covered in this chapter

- Manual lifting
- Lifting using mechanical means
- Lifting equipment register and certification
- Lifting equipment – pre use checks
- Operators certificate
- Signal men
- Standard lifting appliance hand signals
- Safe working load (SWL)
- Problems encountered when lifting where trim is a factor

The incorrect manual lifting of heavy loads results in many injuries, particularly back-related problems. Consequently, wherever possible, the manual lifting of heavy objects should be avoided. If, however, they are undertaken, then this should only be attempted by persons trained in manual lifting procedures. Due consideration should be given to prevailing conditions, the size and shape of the load, and the location of potential hazards, for instance stairs, steps, and hatch ways. If there is ever any doubt, seek advice and assistance. Do not attempt to lift something that is too heavy. Wherever practicable, boxes should be opened and the contents separated to enable easier lifting. Care should be taken to avoid protruding nails, fastenings when lifting packages or boxes.

The secret to safe lifting is posture. The correct procedure to carry out manual lifting is to crouch in front of the load, with feet a little apart to ensure a straight lift. With knees bent and with a straight back the lift is undertaken by the leg muscles, the strongest muscles in the body, consequently injury should be avoided. It should be remembered that the procedure for lowering loads is equally important and should be a reverse operation of lifting. When carrying loads the person completing the lift should ensure the load is not so big as to obscure safe vision.

Wherever possible, lifting by mechanical means should be adopted. Yet, despite years of warnings highlighting the dangers, far too many accidents and injuries result from lifting appliance related incidents. Trolleys and pallet trucks can be used for

Beer
Beer
Beer
Beer
Beer

Beer
Beer
Beer

transporting items too heavy for individuals to lift, but only by competent personnel. In any case, they should only be used when the vessel is in still water and not subject to excessive trim, for example when discharging tankers.

Legislation gives definite guidelines and instructions on lifting operations setting out details about lifting appliances, equipment and testing but all too often these are ignored.

All lifting equipment should be maintained according to manufacturers recommendations, including cranes, hoists, chain blocks, handy billies and snatch blocks.

A lifting equipment register should be implemented and regularly updated. The register should record the history of all lifting equipment from the day it is brought on board to the time of its disposal. The register will be a means for storing certificates of manufacture, test certificates, recording maintenance and dates of disposal. The upkeep of the register would typically be the responsibility of the chief officer who should sign all entries and ensure that certificates, tests and maintenance are kept up to date.

A central location should be identified on the ship for the storage of all lifting appliances and associated equipment. This will include all strops, shackles, wires and lifting eyes as well as chain blocks, handy billies etc. This equipment should be checked regularly by a trained and competent person and always before use.

All personnel should be aware of the correct, safe operation of lifting equipment. They should also be given adequate on board training prior to being assessed as to their ability to use such equipment. When considered suitably accomplished an onboard 'Lifting Appliance Operators' Certificate' should be issued to appropriate personnel which would be valid until their repatriation at the end of their tour on board. As part of the test before a certificate can be issued, personnel should be tested on the hand signals code included in the book on Page 40.

The safe working load (SWL) of any lifting appliance should be clearly marked on the equipment and this should never be exceeded. If there is any doubt, the lift should not be attempted. In the event that conditions change during a lifting operation, the new conditions should be evaluated and operations suspended if necessary.

Personnel should never be lifted by mechanical means other than lifts designed for carrying personnel. All lifting appliances should be secured and locked in position when not in service. Such locking arrangements must, of course, be released prior to use.

When ships' cranes or derricks are employed for discharge of cargo, it is vital that loads are within the equipment safe working load limits and that limiting angles, rotation limits, etc., are not exceeded. Lifting appliances should not be used to drag loads from awkward positions. If necessary, a lead block should be employed, such that forces acting on lifting appliances are vertical.

Whenever a lift is being undertaken, a 'signal man' should be employed who should ensure he is always in visual contact with crane / lift operator, the lift all and other personnel involved in the lift.

When lifting heavy components during maintenance, for example main engine piston changes, it should be remembered that excessive trim changes can have a major impact on safety.

CODE OF HAND SIGNALS

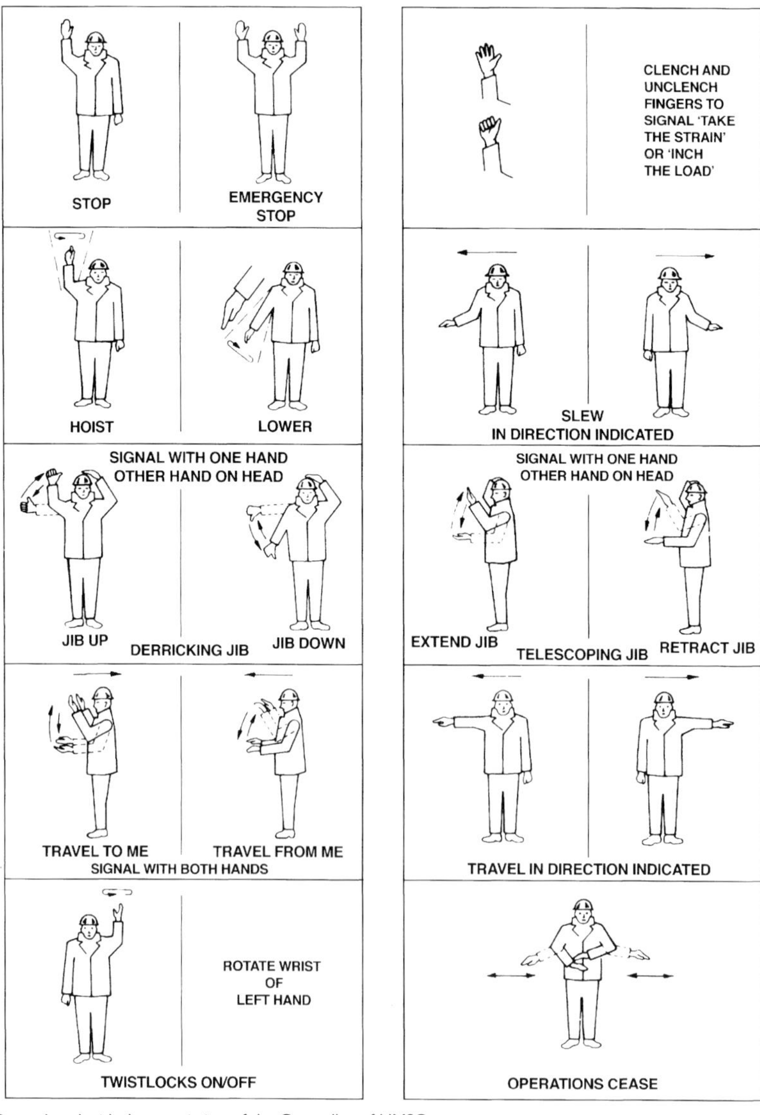

Reproduced with the permission of the Controller of HMSO.

CHAPTER 11

FIRE – PRECAUTIONS, DRILLS AND EMERGENCY PROCEDURES

Topics covered in this chapter

- Welding / hot work
- Oil leaks and spills
- Galley fires
- Smoking onboard ship
- Electrical fires
- Incinerators
- Fire drills and exercises
- Fire – emergency response

Fire is probably one of the most feared and dangerous single events on board ship. Without doubt prevention is always better than cure.

The causes of shipboard fires vary but more common causes include: welding and hot work, oil leaks or spills, galleys, smoking, electrical problems and increasingly incinerators. Particular care should be taken when working in or on these areas. Each of these categories will be considered. This list is not exhaustive but covers principal causation categories.

WELDING / HOT WORK

This is covered in more detail in Chapter 12. Suffice to say that this type of work should be carefully planned, with due consideration given to the risk of fire and only when a hot work permit has been issued.

OIL LEAKS AND SPILLS

These are a potentially serious source of fire and particular care should be taken to avoid spills when transferring diesel oil, bunkers and lubricating oils. This applies whether transfers are from shore, barge or internal. If any leaks are detected they should be rectified immediately and the use of catch pots as an alternative to repair should be avoided.

✓

✗

Many shipboard engine room fires result from the failure of high pressure fuel / lubricating oil lines, whereby high pressure oil is sprayed onto hot surfaces such as exhaust manifolds. All high pressure lines should be regularly checked and any copper washers on these systems should be annealed (heat treated) prior to fitting. On vessels operating with Unmanned Machinery Spaces (UMS) all pressure fuel lines should be sheathed and fitted with leakage collection tanks. These tanks should have level alarms fitted which will initiate an alarm to warn the duty engineer of a potential fuel leak. It is good practice to fit such systems even on vessels not operating UMS.

All exhaust manifolds and hot surfaces capable of providing an ignition source should be properly lagged and sheet metal shrouds fitted.

As mentioned previously the use of catch pots, tundishes and 'temporary' save-alls should be avoided.

GALLEYS

Galleys are another potential source of fire and should always be given careful attention. The galley is considered in more detail in Chapter 9.

SMOKING

Smoking is a very real fire hazard and this should be borne in mind by all smokers. It is particularly important that cigarettes, matches and so on are disposed of carefully. Safety ashtrays with slots to ensure that a cigarette is extinguished are available.

The adoption of designated smoking areas is strongly recommended and, on some ships compulsory. Clear company guidelines should be established. Ships' staff smoking in their accommodation should exercise caution and smoking in bed should be prohibited.

'No smoking' signs should be clearly posted in all areas of a ship where smoking is prohibited.

ELECTRICAL

Electrical problems and faults can easily lead to shipboard fires and any work on electrical systems should only be attempted by competent personnel. If any electrical faults are suspected they should be brought to the attention of appropriate persons and the systems should be isolated. No portable appliances should be left connected to the power supply when not in use. This includes personal stereos, videos, televisions, toasters and similar appliances, as well as electrically driven tools. All electrical equipment should be regularly checked, including personal equipment, and shipboard electrical systems should be subject to regular insulation tests by competent personnel.

INCINERATORS

Incinerators are another potential cause of fire and this is partly due to their increased use on board ship as a result of recent legislation regarding garbage disposal. Incinerators should be protected by fire detection systems. A build up of combustible waste around the incinerator awaiting incineration should be avoided. In fact segregated garbage should be stowed away from the incinerator and only taken there when it is to be incinerated. Particular care should be taken with oily rags, sawdust and waste impregnated with oil due to the risk from spontaneous combustion. Aerosol cans and batteries should not be incinerated as there is a potential risk of explosion. Such items should be retained on board until they can be safely landed ashore.

FIRE DRILLS AND EXERCISES

If, despite the adoption of carefully considered precautions, a fire does start on board ship, the ship's complement must be capable of extinguishing the fire. Thus, training drills and familiarity with equipment is of paramount importance. Sea staff should, whenever possible, attend shore-based fire fighting training courses. Indeed, under some flag states this is a mandatory requirement. The courses can create realism and authenticity within the safety of a shore-based training establishment. Ship's staff must be confident and competent in their ability to fight a shipboard fire. Even if shore assistance is possible, the ship's staff are usually first on the scene.

Drills should be as realistic as possible, but it must be remembered that many injuries occur during drills which have not be carefully planned, with detailed scenarios prepared. Under many administrations, musters and drills are mandatory. However, to maximise their usefulness, particular effort should be put into these drills, rather than simple attendance.

Clear mustering arrangements should be established, fire parties, breathing apparatus (BA) parties and other relevant equipment should be identified and their use practised.

Within the scope of this book it is not possible to consider all types of vessel, crew sizes and equipment levels but each vessel should establish clear guidelines and procedures. At the very least, alarms, fire fighting equipment and communications should be tested and proved during fire drills. All personnel should be familiar with the correct use of all fire fighting appliances, extinguishers, clothing and breathing apparatus. Which extinguishers to use in which fire scenario must be well understood. Fixed installations including fire pumps, emergency fire pumps, flooding systems, ventilation systems, BA bottle compressors, etc., should be regularly tested and maintained in accordance with statutory, manufacturers and classification society requirements.

FIRE – EMERGENCY RESPONSE

If a fire breaks out on board ship immediate reactions can be critical. If you discover a fire, however small, raise the alarm – if you can extinguish the fire using a portable extinguisher or other immediate means do so – but only after raising the alarm. The actions taken in the first few minutes after a fire is discovered are critical and the correct actions must be taken. All personnel should muster and a headcount should be conducted. All supplies of air to the space should be eliminated, as should any fuel or oil supplies which may feed the fire. Remote stops and quick closing valves should be operated as required and as directed by senior officers.

If a space is smoke filled it should be evacuated except by staff wearing breathing apparatus. If a fixed fire fighting installation covers a space, this should be operated as soon as practicable. The decision to use these fixed installations lies with the senior officers on board ship. Care must be taken to ensure that no personnel are unaccounted for and that the operation of the fixed installation will not endanger lives if there is anyone unaccounted for.

When a fire is thought to be extinguished, the space should be inspected by personnel familiar with that space wearing breathing apparatus sets. Care should be taken to prevent the possibility of the fire restarting. When spaces are re-ventilated, extreme care should be taken and the space should be fully ventilated and the atmosphere tested before non-BA wearers re-enter.

Certain fires should be treated using particular procedures. This especially applies to oil fires, chemical fires, uptake fires and cargo fires. Personnel actively involved in these areas should be familiar with the correct response and method of attack – it may save lives.

Dedicated waterproof receptacles containing important emergency response information should be positioned around the vessel, typically in the same location as the international fire connection. Both should be clearly identified and ALWAYS located as indicated.

The emergency / response box should contain

- fire response plans
- details of fire fighting equipment, its location and operation
- safety documents
- ship construction plans
- cargo manifests and stowage plans
- muster lists

and any other details considered appropriate. This information can be used by shore-based personnel who may be asked to assist as required.

It must be remembered that many materials on board ship may give off toxic fumes. This includes items such as furnishings, plastics, clothing and accommodation materials.

CHAPTER 12

WELDING AND BURNING (HOT WORK)

Topics covered in this chapter

- Personal protective equipment requirements when welding
- Welding procedures
- Electric arc welding
- Gas welding
- Burning
- Flame cutting

All welding or burning (hot work) conducted outside the vessel's workshop should only take place when a valid work permit has been issued and the job has been carefully planned. When welding is undertaken in the engine room workshop this should be confined to the welding bay wherever possible. The welding area should be closed off by a fire proof curtain to prevent other workshop users being subjected to the potential hazards of arc eye. Only persons fully competent in the use of this equipment should be allowed to carry out such work.

At the work planning stage, personal protective equipment requirements should be identified. It is recommended that this should include the basic safety equipment plus

- welding goggles / hand-held welding visor or full visor (approved for the type of welding being carried out)
- leather or fire-resistant gloves or gauntlets
- leather or fire-resistant apron
- leather or fire-resistant gaiters
- all such clothing should be oil free – welders should never work whilst standing in water or whilst wearing damp or wet clothing.

When the personal protective equipment required by the operator has been established, the work space should be inspected and all potential hazards identified. All potentially combustible debris in the area should he removed and areas thoroughly cleaned of oils and grease. If there is a risk of sparks, etc., passing through hatches, stairs or gratings they should be closed off. No hot work should be attempted in the vicinity of bunker or oil storage tanks unless they have been

PAINT

drained, cleaned and proved free of flammable gases and continually vented.

Stand-by men should be employed to monitor both the immediate area and the operator as well as adjacent spaces behind bulkheads and areas above or below decks. Where necessary stand-by men should wear the same protective equipment as the operator. They should isolate the power supply if anything untoward occurs.

Appropriate fire extinguishers should be at the site and methods of raising fire alarms clearly established. If it is necessary to isolate fire detection zones during hot work these should be reinstated at the earliest opportunity. In any event, spaces should be monitored until all risk of fire is eliminated. Typically this should be for a period no less than two hours.

ELECTRIC ARC WELDING EQUIPMENT

This type of equipment is potentially very dangerous. To reduce the potential of electric shock, it is recommended that welding machines should be direct current (DC) machines with outputs limited to a maximum of 70V open circuit. These machines should be limited such that they cannot produce open-circuit idling voltages in excess of 42V. If alternating current machines are used then the idle voltage should be limited to 25V. The function of these limiting devices should be tested and proved prior to using the machine. The equipment, electrode holder,

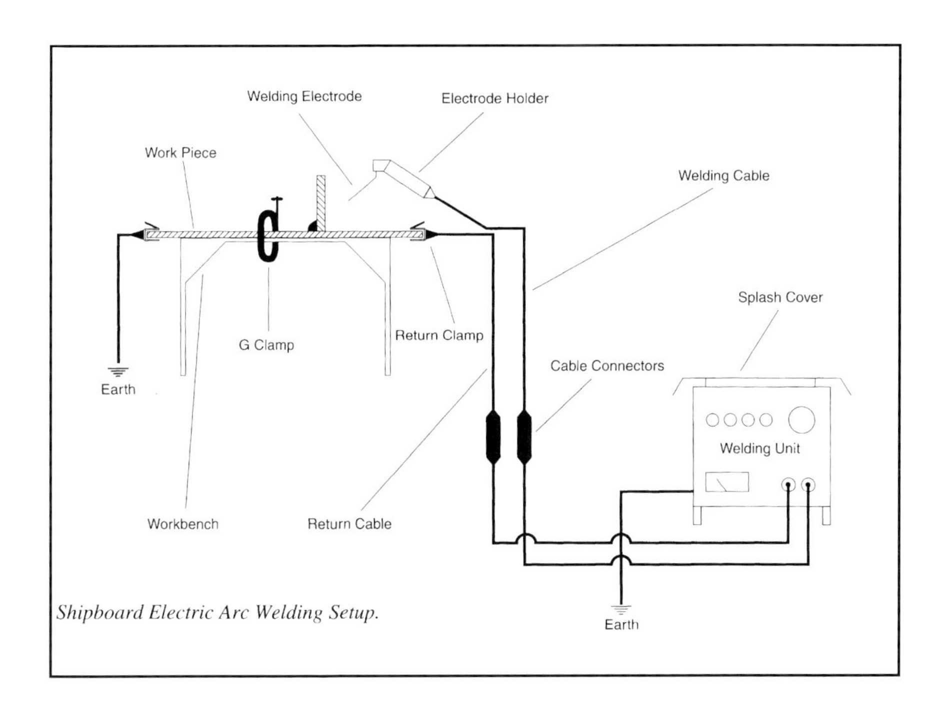

Shipboard Electric Arc Welding Setup.

clamping arrangements and cables, including connectors, should also be checked prior to service. If equipment is deemed faulty it should be removed from service.

A two-cable system should be adopted to avoid potential risks of electrocution and injury. This requires a supply and return cable to the welding set and a separate earth between work piece and the ship's structure. The use of a single cable with full return should be avoided.

Particular care should be taken when changing electrodes to avoid burns and this should only be done with the power source isolated. Hot electrode ends should be carefully disposed of, not simply thrown to the deck. Spare electrodes should be kept in an electrode oven to keep them dry and ready for use. Care should be taken when removing 'slag' from the work piece and goggles capable of protecting the eyes from flying 'slag' should be used. Welding goggles / visors are not always designed for this duty.

GAS WELDING, BURNING AND FLAME CUTTING

This is also a potentially dangerous activity and care should be taken when conducting such work.

Oxygen and acetylene should be stored in separate bottle rooms which should be protected by both fire detection and fire extinguishing systems. The rooms should be well ventilated and all bottles should be secured and clamped. No smoking signs should be clearly posted. Grease should not be used on bottle valves or connection threads. The regulators, fittings, etc., for oxygen and acetylene are usually different sizes and of different hand threads. Fixed pipe-work, for example from bottle rooms to workshops, etc., should be colour coded: blue for oxygen and red for acetylene. Bottle numbers and pressures should be recorded and monitored, and protective caps should be fitted to all bottles not in use. Flame arrestors should be fitted in supply lines, usually fitted on the low-pressure side of the regulator, and they should be maintained in good order. Bottle supply valves should be shut when the equipment is not in use and gas bottles should only be changed by competent persons.

Manufacturers' recommended pressures for welding or burning should be closely adhered to and maximum pressures must never be exceeded.

CHAPTER 13

ACCESS, TRANSIT AND DISEMBARKING

Topics covered in this chapter

- Access to and from the ship
- Transit around the ship
- Safe access routes
- Shipboard slips and falls

From the moment any person sets foot on a ship's accommodation ladder they should be aware that they are entering a potentially hazardous area. This message should be clearly indicated at the bottom of the gangway with personal protective equipment requirements, smoking regulations and restricted access information clearly displayed.

Maritime administrations place an obligation on ship owners (and their shipboard representative – the master) to provide a safe means of access to and from the vessel. This is usually complied with by using an accommodation ladder. It is imperative that the accommodation ladder or gangway is correctly rigged, adjusted to suit the prevailing conditions, well lit and easily accessible. A safety net, correctly adjusted, should always be fitted. If access is by means of shore facilities it is usually the responsibility of the master to ensure it is correctly rigged. The safe working load and maximum number of persons allowed on an accommodation ladder must be clearly marked and never exceeded.

If access to the vessel is by gangway, gangplank or rope ladder they must be safely rigged, well lit and in compliance with appropriate legislation.

Life-buoys with line and quoit attached should be available at all points of access to the vessel and should be of the type with self / water activated lights.

Extreme care should be taken when embarking and disembarking any vessel. Whenever a ladder or other means of access is being rigged the personnel involved should wear the basic safety equipment considered the norm as well as additional safety gear, including safety harnesses and buoyancy aids.

Safe access and transit routes around the ship should be clearly marked either as painted lines on the deck or by using safety tape. These safe routes should avoid hazards such as cargo lifts, stores lifts, operations, machinery spaces or pump rooms, etc. On vessels where cargo operations move around the vessel, tape is a better option as it can be moved so as to allow access avoiding ongoing cargo work.

OIL

Decks should be kept clear, as far as possible, of cargo, debris, tools and similar obstructions, and all potential tripping hazards such as securing lugs, sounding pipes, Butterworth lids and pad eyes should be painted in a contrasting colour to highlight the hazard. Personnel visiting the vessel, including pilots, superintendents, supernumeraries and shore workers, should be escorted on board by a responsible member of the ship's crew and guided to their destination to avoid hazards. Hard hats should be kept at the top of the gangway in case people arrive without their own. Any ladders, stairways and access routes should be well maintained and well lit. Indeed, all lighting should be regularly checked, particularly prior to arrival in port.

If access is required to holds, cargo spaces and the like, for example by surveyors or inspectors, then all the potential hazards should be pointed out and the correct personal protective equipment donned. If the ship owner's requirements are not met by visiting personnel then access should be denied until the situation is rectified.

Whatever the reason may be for individuals being on board ship, they must always be aware of potential hazards and proceed with caution. Common sense should prevail, as slips and falls cause some 45% of personal injuries.

Far too many injuries, even fatalities, happen when personnel are embarking or disembarking vessels. **So, take care!**

WORK SAFELY
PREVENT ACCIDENTS
2S

NO SMOKIN

CHAPTER 14

ENTRY INTO ENCLOSED SPACES

Topics covered in this chapter

- What is an enclosed space?
- Entry permits
- Entry procedures
- Rescue from an enclosed space
- Marine safety card
- Atmosphere testing
- Testing for oxygen deficiency
- Testing for the presence of flammable gases or vapours
- Testing for toxic gases

Despite the fact that the hazards are well known, far too many accidents, injuries and fatalities result from entry into enclosed or dangerous spaces. An enclosed or dangerous space is one which has, or may have, an oxygen deficiency, explosive atmosphere, toxic atmosphere, or when the condition of the atmosphere is unknown. It is not possible to list all such spaces which may be present onboard ship, but such a list must include

- cargo holds or tanks
- deep tanks
- void spaces
- tanker pump rooms
- gas carrier compressor rooms
- double bottoms
- duct keels
- ballast tanks
- sewage storage or treatment tanks
- inert gas rooms (including scrubbers, etc.)
- battery lockers
- storage rooms for fixed fire fighting mediums (i.e. CO_2 and halon)
- pressure vessels (including air receivers and boilers, etc.)
- cofferdams

- cable and pipe trunks
- chain lockers
- incinerators and boiler furnaces
- refrigeration compressor and gas spaces
- bunker, diesel and oil tanks
- gas carrier void spaces.

Any space which has been battened down without full ventilation should be considered an enclosed space or dangerous space and entry must only be made after careful planning and job explanation. Moreover, all safety procedures should have been complied with and an entry permit issued. The atmosphere should be tested and proved safe for access.

As a general rule any space, where the condition of that space is or is suspected of being unable to support human life, should be tested prior to entry. The space should be fully ventilated and the ventilation continued throughout any period of entry. When and only when the atmosphere is proven safe should entry be made without breathing apparatus. Entry should only be made using breathing apparatus when it is impossible to ventilate the space or when a rescue is to be attempted.

Many people have been killed over the years trying to rescue a friend or colleague – always remember – if the space will not support them why should it keep you alive. In such circumstances rescues should only be attempted when rescuers are wearing breathing apparatus. The rescue should be well coordinated, controlled and rescue teams should be well practised.

Enclosed spaces are often difficult to access and poorly lit, thus every attempt should be made to make access safe and the areas should be well lit. Often this will require the use of suitably certificated intrinsically safe equipment either torches or portable lighting.

Personal atmosphere testing equipment which can easily be worn is available and such equipment can constantly monitor any space within which the wearer is operating.

The North of England P&I Association has distributed to its Members a marine safety card *Entry Into Enclosed Spaces*. If they have not already done so, ship owners may care to consider adopting this form and incorporating it into their own Safety Management System. The checklist sets out the appropriate safety checks which must be completed prior to entry into an enclosed space and should be considered to be the minimum standard. The checklist should be completed by the master or responsible officer as well as the person who is to enter the space. A copy of the marine safety card appears on page 58.

NORTH OF ENGLAND –
ENTRY INTO ENCLOSED SPACES CHECKLIST

Note: Please check and ensure that your own Safety Management System includes an official checklist to be used for entry into enclosed spaces – this form is presented as one example incorporating industry best practice

Section One (to be checked by master or responsible officer)

- The space should be properly ventilated, tested and found safe.
- Ventilation should be continued throughout occupancy of the space.
- The space should be tested regularly during occupancy.
- Rescue and resuscitation equipment should be available at the entrance.
- A responsible person should be stationed at the entrance.
- A system of communication should be agreed – such equipment must be of an approved type and intrinsically safe.
- Adequate lighting should be provided and be of a type that is appropriate for the duty.

Section Two (to be checked by person entering the space)

This part of the checklist is a check that the person entering the space has received instruction or permission to enter the space, ensures persons entering have checked Section One has been complied with, communications are established between themselves and the stand-by man.

Section Three

Pertains to breathing apparatus, the operation and testing of them, familiarity with their use and any emergency signals.

It is recommended that a safety trolley, or box for vessels where access to main decks is difficult, should be prepared with all the apparatus required for entry into enclosed spaces for rescues stowed within. Thus when entry is to be arranged the contents should be taken to the point of entry ready for use as required. A safety box contents should include as a minimum

- two breathing apparatus
- two spare BA bottles
- safety harnesses / rescue harnesses
- life lines
- two spare torches (suitable for duty i.e. intrinsically safe or as required depending on type of ship, etc.)
- resuscitation equipment
- stretcher.

MARINE SAFETY CARD ENTRY INTO ENCLOSED SPACES

The atmospher
incapable of su
content and/or
applies to tanks

Before entry
tanks, coffe
holds and s
assessment
a responsib

Do not ente
the master
the approp
your ship h
system, wh
this card,
dangerous

The master o
safe to enter
(a) that the
mechanic
(b) that the
appropri
levels of

Where th
suspect i
or when
apparatu

Protectiv
All persons
suitable cl
provided. A
be slipper
helmets p
clothing li
Special cl
with harm
harnesses

Any additi
followed.

Further i
spaces is
for Merch

Issued by
Carthusia
London E

SAFETY CHECK LIST

Before entry into the enclosed space the appropriate safety checks listed below must be carried out by the master or the responsible officer and by the person who is to enter.

NB. For entry into cargo pump rooms only those items in red need to be checked.

Date [ ] Time [ ]

SECTION 1

To be checked ✔ by the master or the responsible officer

1.1 Has the space been properly ventilated, tested and found safe? ☐

1.2 Have arrangements been made to continue ventilation during occupancy of the space and at breaks? ☐

1.3 Have arrangements been made to repeat testing at regular intervals during occupancy and after breaks? ☐

1.4 Are rescue and resuscitation equipment available for immediate use at the entrance to the space? ☐

1.5 Have arrangements been made for a responsible person to be in constant attendance at the entrance to the space? ☐

1.6 Has a system of communication between the person at the entrance and those entering the space been agreed and tested? ☐

1.7 Are access and illumination adequate? ☐

1.8 Are portable lights and other equipment to be used of an appropriate type? ☐

SECTION 2

To be checked ✔ by the person who is to enter the space after the relevant checks in SECTION 1 have been made.

2.1 Have you been given instructions or permission by the master or the responsible officer to enter the space? ☐

2.2 Are you satisfied all relevant checks in SECTION 1 have been completed? ☐

2.3 Do you understand the arrangements made for communication between yourself and the responsible person in attendance at the entrance to the space? ☐

2.4 Are you aware you should leave the space immediately in the event of ventilation problems or communication failure? ☐

SECTION 3

Where breathing apparatus is to be used this section must be checked jointly by the responsible officer and the persons who are to enter the space.

3.1 Are you familiar with the apparatus to be used? ☐

3.2 Has the apparatus been checked as follows?
(i) Adequacy of air supply
(ii) Low pressure audible alarm
(iii) Face mask – air supply and tightness ☐

3.3 Have the emergency signals and other emergency arrangements been agreed? ☐

Where instructions have been given that a responsible person be at the entrance to the space, the persons entering the space should show him their completed card before entering.

The man standing by at the top of the tank should record entry times, advise the wheel house and monitor movements so at all times everyone's whereabouts are known. If at any time the conditions in the space change, the atmosphere becomes suspect or someone feels unwell / appears to be suffering ALL personnel should vacate the space and the full procedure re-done.

ENCLOSED SPACE – ATMOSPHERE TESTING

Before any person enters an enclosed space the atmosphere should be tested. However, the particular tests that will be conducted vary depending on the conditions to which the enclosed space has been subjected. Tests will for instance be different if the space was a ballast tank, cargo hold or fuel tank.

The tests available are for oxygen deficiency, flammable gases and vapours and toxic gases and the tests should always be carried out in that order. Operator should ensure that all meters used for testing are checked and properly calibrated.

TESTING FOR OXYGEN DEFICIENCY

Oxygen deficiency tests should be conducted using a recognised, calibrated and fully certificated oxygen meter. Entry should only be permitted if the percentage oxygen content by volume has given a steady reading greater than 20%. It is good practice to test the atmosphere at several levels in a space, if appropriate, usually at the top, middle and bottom of a tank.

TESTING FOR FLAMMABLE GASES OR VAPOURS

The meter used for this purpose is the combustible gas indicator or 'explosimeter' which can detect the percentage content of the atmosphere of flammable gases and vapours. If for any reason a suitable meter is not available then a space should either be flooded with ballast and then pumped out to induce fresh air in or an external ventilation system must be arranged and the space ventilated for a specified period. This will be dependent on volume air changes.

When lower flammable unit readings fall below 1% then the space can be considered safe for entry. But only when the oxygen reading is at least 20% by volume, and no toxic gases are present.

TESTING FOR TOXIC GASES

On many vessels, especially chemical carriers, crude oil carriers and specialist product tankers, toxic substances may be present in closed cargo spaces. Indeed even vessels carrying toxic cargoes as containerised cargo should have testing facilities on board.

Seemingly innocuous substances can release toxic substances into the environment. Examples include vegetable or animal oils which can release hydrogen sulphide when they come into contact with sea water.

Whenever there is a likelihood or possibility of toxic gases being present, the atmosphere must be tested. Up-to-date internationally accepted exposure level guidelines should be consulted before any entry to a space which may contain toxic gases is considered.

It is important to realise a combustible gas analyser will not be suitable for detecting dangerous levels of toxic gases particularly if they are close to occupational exposure limits. Dangerous levels may well be below flammable limits thus often they will remain undetected without the use of specialised toxic atmosphere testing equipment.

GENERALLY

All atmosphere analysing equipment should be regularly checked and inspected. Carrying cases and straps must also be checked on a regular basis many analysers have been damaged or destroyed after being dropped. Analysers should be regularly calibrated against test equipment and be checked ashore by a shore-based calibration house. Certification must be valid and should be retained onboard. Only people fully trained in the use of such equipment should carry out testing of potentially hazardous spaces.

CHAPTER 15

MOORING AND ANCHORING OPERATIONS

Topics covered in this chapter

- Anchoring
- Mooring operations
- Handling wires and ropes
- Taking a tug

The fairly routine activities of mooring, unberthing and anchoring vessels often lead to serious injuries and even fatalities. With careful planning and suitable training, most of these accidents could have been avoided. The loads and forces experienced in ship's ropes and wires during mooring operations can be considerable and due caution needs to be exercised at all times.

ANCHORING

All personnel involved in anchoring operations should wear the basic personal safety equipment itemised in Chapter 2. Goggles and dust masks should also be worn by all persons in the vicinity to avoid the hazards of flying rust, debris and mud as the anchor and cable is paid out. The anchor should be paid out in a controlled manner, usually on the brake, with continuous communication with the wheel house.

A potential hazard which is not always appreciated is that of sea snakes and although this is not a world-wide problem persons involved in anchoring operations and stowing the anchor should be aware of the potential dangers. Personnel should not stand in line with the cable but should instead stand to one side when letting go or heaving the anchor.

The working areas should be 'anti-slip' and if raised platforms are used, correctly secured gratings are recommended. Guards on windlasses should be secured and in good condition. Power supply lines or pipes for steam, hydraulic oil, etc., should be maintained in good condition, correctly secured and where necessary protected with covers and insulation.

Anchors should be secured for sea with care. The guillotine should be dropped and secured and additional securing wires arranged so as to avoid the

anchors being inadvertently dropped. Spurling pipe covers should be closed and cemented to avoid flooding of chain lockers but this should only be attempted once anchors and cables have been secured.

MOORING OPERATIONS

Considerable care is required with the stowage of wires and ropes as well as the maintenance of roller fairleads, bits, winch drums, brakes and clutches.

Ropes and wires should be regularly inspected and maintained. They should be carefully stowed, preferably off the deck on pallets or the like, and kept away from moisture, chemicals and other substances which may harm them. Ropes and wires should be protected from direct sunlight whether they be stowed on deck or on reels or drums. Wire ropes should be treated with suitable lubricants which should be worked into the core of the wire to avoid the rope drying out.

When handling wires and ropes, seafarers should wear leather-palmed gloves to prevent hand injuries. However when turning ropes on drum ends, extreme care should be exercised as gloves could become entrapped. On such occasions seafarers may wish to remove gloves. Ropes and wires should be flaked out on the deck prior to port arrival and arranged to help the operation go as smoothly as possible. Personnel should never stand in the bight of a rope. Sufficient personnel should be assigned to the mooring operation and one person should be designated as winch / windlass driver.

Whilst responsible for driving the winch he should remain at the control station and in close communication with the officer in charge. All seamen should be aware of the potential hazards and remain in positions of safety whenever possible. Care should be exercised when throwing heaving lines to avoid hitting people with the 'monkey's fist'!

It should be remembered that nylon, polyester and polypropylene ropes, unlike natural fibre ropes, give no audible indication of imminent failure due to overloading. If it appears that ropes are coming under excessive strain the load should be reduced. When a rope is being run on the drum end a maximum of three turns should be used and this should be controlled by one man, with another coiling the rope as it comes off the drum end.

When alongside, the moorings should be constantly monitored and sufficient personnel allocated to tending and adjusting moorings. This is particularly relevant in tidal waters and on vessels with high loading and discharging rates.

On some vessels, mooring operations can be quite awkward, and on others, such as long haul traders, they can be a rare operation. In either case, the operation should be well planned and all personnel involved should be familiar with the proposed sequence of events and what to do in the event of unforeseen circumstances arising.

When making fast a tug it should be remembered that the ship has little control and that the tug can apply load at any time. Wherever possible, ship's lines should be used, as the ship has no control over the condition of a tug's wires or ropes. In some parts of the world, a tug's ropes will be in excellent condition, but this will not always be the case.

In conclusion, good seamanship and the use of the correct personal protective equipment plays a vital role in the prevention of injury during mooring and anchoring operations.

CHAPTER 16

CARGO WORK – HOLDS, HATCHES AND TANKS

Topics covered in this chapter

- Commercial pressures
- Shipowners / shipboard guide to good practice
- Operating hatch covers
- Hold inspections
- Hold ladders
- Potentially dangerous cargoes
- IMDG Code

The carriage of cargo is, of course, the reason merchant ships trade. So, when cargo is being worked there are perceived pressures, as well as real pressures, which may come into play. There may be a temptation to cut corners to achieve deadlines, and to disregard safe practices. This may lead to mistakes being made, which in turn may lead to accidents and injuries which should have been avoided.

Cargo work and the period alongside are often very busy times and occasionally unexpected events occur. Therefore, it is vital that the whole operation is fully discussed and correctly planned. If an unexpected task arises then an unscheduled work plan should be prepared. Shore workers, stevedores and the like should be briefed on safe practices and owners' recommended guidelines. Surveyors should be briefed on shipboard safety and rather than being left to roam the ship, entering holds, tanks, and so on, at will, they should only be allowed to transit the ship if accompanied by a member of the ship's complement. All visitors should wear the minimum basic safety equipment – at least boilersuits, steel toe capped shoes and hard hats. Also, of course, only safe routes of access should be used.

The improper operation of hatches and hatch covers has been the cause of many injuries. It is vital that all personnel involved in the operation of hatch covers are familiar with their operation and the potential risks involved. Maintenance, inspections and testing should be carried out in accordance with manufacturer's instructions. Whenever hatch covers are being operated all personnel should remain clear of the hatches. If visibility is a problem then the operator should

RESTRICTED
ACCESS

maintain radio contact with all persons assisting him. No-one should climb on hatch covers unless they are properly secured. If at any time there is a risk of a fall, or when personnel are working more than 2m above the deck, safety harnesses should be worn. On vessels with non-mechanical hatch covers and pontoons, extreme care should be taken when lifting and manoeuvring beams, pontoons, boards or slabs. At no time should personnel stand under lifts. All components should be marked to ensure correct re-assembly.

Cargo holds or tanks must be inspected on a regular basis. Despite the heavy workload on board, the correct procedures should always be followed. If spaces have been closed, then the formal entry into enclosed space procedures must be followed. This applies to shore personnel and ship's personnel alike. Care should be taken when using hold or tank ladders and these areas should be adequately lit. Even when spaces are proven gas free and safe for entry, a stand-by man should be positioned at the point of entry. Procedures for emergency responses should be established and practised during emergency drills. (See Chapter 14 for further details on entry into enclosed spaces).

Hold access ladders should be well maintained, clean and fitted with safety guardrails in good order. This is particularly important on bulk carriers where these ladders are susceptible to damage during loading and discharging.

During cargo work, transit up the deck should always be on the non-cargo-working side of the ship. On vessels working both sides, at anchor to barges for example, transit up or down the deck should only be attempted when a lift is not going on overhead.

If a cargo is to be loaded which is considered dangerous, or even if its characteristics are unknown to the master and his crew, then reference should be made to the International Maritime Dangerous Goods Code (IMDG Code). If the potential risks are still in doubt, then the master / owners should seek further advice. Some cargoes may appear quite innocuous but, in fact, may pose extreme danger. For example logs and scrap metal may cause a serious oxygen deficiency within a cargo compartment. Lives have been lost because this fact was not appreciated. Coal cargoes can generate sufficient quantities of methane gas to produce a very serious risk of explosion.

The message must be – if in doubt, check it out.

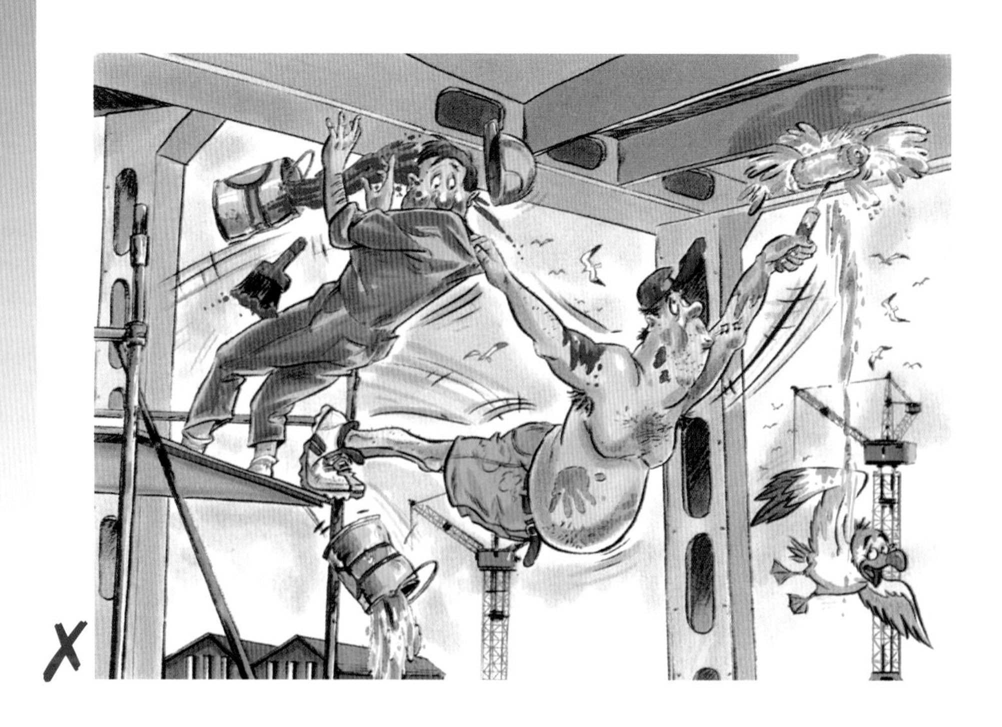

CHAPTER 17

OTHER AREAS NOT SPECIFICALLY COVERED

Topics covered in this chapter

- Areas not covered in a separate chapter
- Asbestos
- Passengers
- Accident reporting
- Dealing with an incident

It is only by adopting best practices that the potential dangers inherent in working onboard ship can be kept under control, and accidents and injuries avoided.

So long as personnel remember the potential dangers and conscientiously act against them, the number and severity of injuries can be greatly reduced. Every action on board ship can affect safety and when things go wrong the consequences can be horrendous.

Many injuries happen as the result of over familiarity, cutting corners and commercial pressures. As such, they often could have been avoided. Others happen during boat drills and exercises, sometimes with catastrophic results. Several seafarers have lost their lives in recent years in lifeboat drills or whilst attempting to lower life boats – don't add to the number.

Simple things demand attention. Clearing up minor leaks, checking procedures, and similar routine actions, can have an immediate impact.

Some areas have not been directly considered in this guide to good practice but must be planned and thought through if injuries are to be avoided. They include

- bunkering operations*
- working aloft
- painting and spraying
- testing and launching lifeboats
- transferring and loading lubricants
- helicopter operations
- tank and hold cleaning operations

- communications and radar equipment
- rigging of cranes and derricks
- working overside
- watertight doors
- vehicle operations
- breathing apparatus and resuscitation equipment
- using high pressure washers
- steam and hydraulics
- working with shore-based personnel
- cargo treatment, fumigation, etc.
- intrinsically safe equipment
- abrasive wheels.

* More detailed information is contained in *Bunker Claims Prevention – A Guide to Good Practice*, published by North of England.

If the same safety philosophies discussed in this guide are adopted during the tasks identified above, personal injuries will hopefully be avoided.

ASBESTOS

Another area that must be considered is asbestosis. Asbestos was used extensively in the shipbuilding industry for many years. Dust fibres produced by asbestos are very small, but may cause serious illness / injury including lung cancer.

Any work involving asbestos should only be carried out by approved specialist contractors.

PASSENGERS

Many vessels are built to carry a live cargo, a human cargo – passengers. However, many personal injury claims arise when passengers are injured. The prevention of passenger personal injury is outside the intended scope of this loss prevention guide suffice to say that passengers should be reminded that ships are potentially dangerous environments and not simply floating hotels. Ships invariably move in a seaway, passenger ships do roll and many passengers suffer slips and falls as they are not used to a ship's movement.

Officers and crew serving onboard passenger ships and ferries should be particularly aware of the potentially problematic nature of their cargo and should provide assistance and advice as necessary.

ACCIDENT REPORTING

Although not specifically included in this guide to Personal Injury Prevention the importance of accident reporting and investigation cannot be over emphasised.

The reporting and investigation of incidents, near misses and injuries helps further identify risks. After investigation, information can be promulgated in an effort to make personnel that may be exposed to similar risk more aware.

We must learn from the experiences of others.

Incidents should be investigated quickly and thoroughly. As far as possible, conjecture and opinion should be avoided.

DEALING WITH AN INCIDENT

In the sad event of injuries on board, they should be dealt with as professionally and efficiently as possible, using the contents of the medical locker as required. The locker should be well stocked with medicines identified by world administrations. If injuries are severe, or ships officers require medical advice, help should be sought as soon as possible. If treating injured personnel, protective equipment to prevent the contraction of AIDS, hepatitis and similar illnesses should be used. Such equipment includes disposable rubber gloves and clothing covers. If artificial respiration is necessary, then this should only be attempted whilst using a Brook Airway or similar preventative shields.

Accidents should be fully investigated and safety reviewed in an attempt to avoid further similar accidents. The collecting of evidence, how to investigate an incident and accident reporting is outside the scope of this publication.

Be safe – beware – be here

STOP!

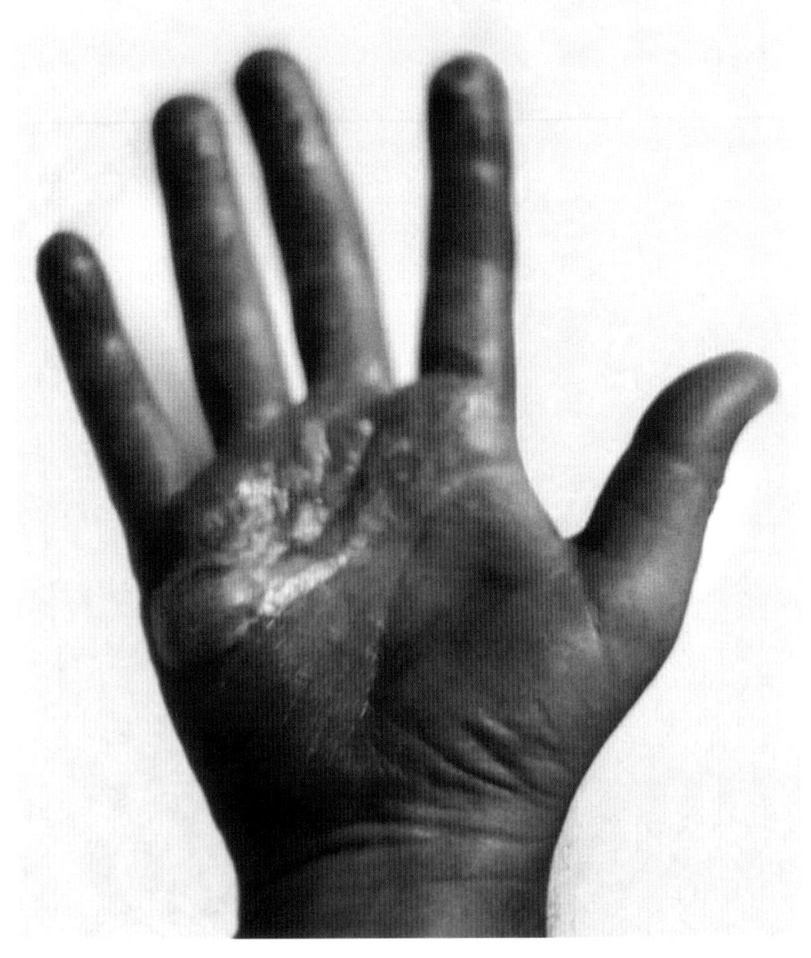

Safety is in your HANDS!

CHAPTER 18

CASE STUDIES – PERSONAL INJURY CLAIMS

1. PERSONAL PROTECTIVE EQUIPMENT

The incident

A young fourth engineer was asked by the second engineer to treat the boiler water with chemicals during his watch. Although unfamiliar with the chemicals or the task in hand, the fourth engineer agreed to take on the task.

What happened?

The job was allocated without prior planning as the second engineer had simply been unable to treat the boiler on his watch due to lack of time and his heavy workload. On the ship in question, boiler treatment was in a powder form. The established procedure was to add chemical to feed water and then feed this chemical mixture to the boiler via a feed dosage pot.

The fourth engineer, unfamiliar with the procedure, added the water to the chemical. The subsequent reaction caused chemical to be splashed into the fourth engineer's left eye.

The situation was exacerbated because the fourth engineer, not realising the potential hazard, did not use the personal protective equipment which had been provided on board and was readily available.

What went wrong?

The task in hand was not properly planned, the hazards were not fully identified and the correct protective equipment was not used. The fourth engineer was not familiar with the correct procedures and was not instructed or supervised. As a result of his injuries, he was blinded in one eye and was unable to continue his chosen career.

What can we learn from this incident?

Correct planning, training and preparation is vital if a task is to be completed successfully and safely. All staff must be familiar with the correct personal protective equipment available and required for the task in hand. All personnel should be aware of how to react in the event of such an incident.

2. GOOD HOUSEKEEPING

The incident

A crew member working in the engine room fell through an unmarked opening in the engine room floor plates.

What happened?

The vessel was at sea and undertaking a heavy programme of planned maintenance with all engine room personnel very busy. A newly appointed engineer cadet was assigned to engine room familiarisation and line tracing. This was as much in an effort to keep him 'out of the way' as it was to enhance his on board training. He was not familiar with the vessel or with on board safety procedures but left to his own devices.

The cadet traced a section of seawater main to the bottom plates where it then disappeared under them. In his efforts to trace the line the cadet simply lifted the appropriate section of floor plate and continued his efforts. An engine room oiler walking around the corner of the main engine fell down the unmarked opening. He sustained serious leg injuries including a compound fracture of his right femur. The oiler had to be stretchered from the engine room and then air-lifted to a shore hospital where he underwent an operation to rectify his injuries.

What went wrong?

Due to the high workload on board, the cadet was not correctly instructed or advised of the correct safe procedures to be adopted. The cadet's duties were not highlighted on the work plan and other engine room staff were unaware of the line tracing being undertaken. In all cases where floor plates, gratings and hatches are removed and openings made in decks these openings should be clearly marked using safety tape or ropes. Where possible secure fencing should be employed.

What can we learn from this incident?

Even in times of high workload ALL tasks must be carefully planned. Work plans must be circulated, all personnel must be familiar with procedures and safety guidelines and people should only be asked to attempt duties for which they are suitably trained. Everyone should be aware of the work being undertaken on board at any given time. Correct planning is fundamental to prevention.

3. WORK ON ELECTRICAL EQUIPMENT

The incident

A vessel arrived at its load port and prepared to load cargo. The vessel was a general cargo vessel built in the 1980's. Number 3 crane was not working properly and a crew member saw flames emitting from the crane power supply. The ship's electrician was called and during his efforts to rectify faults he was electrocuted.

What happened?

After being called to attend the inoperative crane, the chief engineer and electrician isolated the power supply and began trying to locate the fault. The chief engineer left the crane to obtain a portable light and returned to find the electrician fatally injured. It transpired that although the 440V power supply had been isolated, the 220V control and lighting supply had not. The electrician died from 220V electrocution.

What went wrong?

The attempted repairs to the crane motor were badly planned, the potential hazards were not identified and a permit to work system was not adopted. The correct safety procedures were ignored with tragic consequences.

What can we learn from this incident?

It is vital that tasks are correctly planned. However it is particularly vital when working on electrical equipment that correct procedures are adopted.

Electrical drawings should be consulted and full isolation provided and then the equipment should be tested with a suitable multimeter to ensure that no electrical power remains. Circuit breakers should be locked, all fuses removed and danger notices posted. The chief engineer should then ensure all aspects of the permit to work system are complied with prior to signing and allowing the work to proceed.

Whenever any personnel are working on electrical equipment they should be accompanied by a colleague who can react in the event of problems. Such personnel should be familiar with the response required when people suffer electric shock as detailed earlier in this guide.

Insulated tools and equipment should be used and electrically insulated rubber gloves should be worn as necessary.

4. WELDING AND BURNING (HOT WORK)

The incident

A welder working in the cargo hold of a vessel was engulfed in flames after a dust explosion and suffered extensive injuries

What happened?

The welder was involved in removing large sections of steel work in a cargo hold of the entered vessel. A large section of steel which had been burnt out fell to the bottom of the cargo hold which had previously been used for carrying grain and fishmeal. The impact caused dust collected in the hold bottom and on frames to form a dust cloud. When this dust cloud made contact with the welder's welding flame the dust exploded and the welder was engulfed in a fire ball. His oily dirty clothes caught fire and he suffered extensive burns to 60% of his body.

What went wrong?

This tragic incident is a classic example of poor safety planning, inappropriate supervision and failure to follow established safety procedures. The potential risks of explosion of grain and fishmeal dust are well known yet hot work was permitted without

- careful and thorough cleaning of the cargo hold
- a gas free – hot work permit being issued
- a clear work plan being established and promulgated
- correct personal protective equipment being worn
- a fire watch and fire extinguishing systems being arranged.

What can we learn from this incident?

Whenever hot work is to be conducted it is vital correct planning and procedures are adopted. Before a hot work permit is issued all the potential hazards must be identified and eliminated. Even when the dangers are not obviously apparent they should be investigated. If the master or members of the crew are not familiar with cargoes carried they should seek advice.

All working clothes should be maintained as clean as possible and oil free and the correct protective equipment must be worn. Although unlikely to have stopped all the injuries in this case the use of fire resistant suits, gauntlets and gaiters may have reduced the scale of injuries suffered by the welder.

The use of the correct personal protective equipment and by adopting safe, well planned procedures many injuries can be prevented.

5. ENTRY INTO ENCLOSED SPACES

The incident

A crew member attempting to take hold temperatures and gas readings from a cargo hold on a vessel carrying steam coal was killed.

What happened?

The vessel, a Panamax bulk carrier, loaded a full cargo of steam coal for discharge in Northern Europe. On the voyage to Europe, the owner's instructions were to take gas and temperature readings of all cargo holds on a daily basis. As the vessel was not fitted with a fixed sampling system it was to be done via access hatches / ventilators using rubber tubing. The ventilation system was shut down once the methane levels began to rise.

These readings were normally taken by the senior rating. On this occasion he was busy, so the third officer volunteered to take the readings. He assured the chief officer he knew what he was doing. What happened next is unclear but he was discovered unconscious in an access trunking by the chief officer. The chief officer advised the wheel house and then attempted to rescue the third officer. The body of the third officer and the unconscious chief officer were removed by crew in breathing apparatus.

The third officer was pronounced dead but the chief officer was revived by resuscitation methods using a Brook Airway. He was transferred by helicopter to a nearby warship where he recovered full health.

What went wrong?

Once again, a change in circumstance led to a person, attempting duties with which he was unfamiliar, being injured. Tragically in this case a fatality was the result. The job was not properly planned, no unplanned work permit was issued and the operation was badly supervised.

Firstly, nobody should enter an enclosed space without full ventilation of the space and full compliance with the checklist on the marine safety card – Entry Into Enclosed Spaces.

Secondly, if a rescue from an enclosed space is to be attempted, this must be well co-coordinated and safely conducted. Entry without the aid of breathing apparatus must be avoided at all cost. There is no reason to think that the atmosphere which overcame the victim will not have the same effect on the rescuer.

All personnel on board ship should be aware of the potential risks associated with the cargo being carried and relevant safety considerations.

On this particular ship with its large open areas of deck the use of a purpose built safety trolley could have been adopted and used to attempt the rescue.

What can we learn from this incident?

Personnel should only attempt duties for which they are trained and fully competent. If that competence is in doubt more careful supervision must be arranged. ALL tasks must be fully planned and correct procedures established.

Entry into enclosed spaces must be in compliance with recognised procedures and when the marine safety card has been completed. Other factors raised in this guide should be given full consideration.

The testing of such cargo spaces should only be attempted by competent personnel using remote methods such as hoses etc. and they should never be asked to work alone.

Any personnel attempting the rescue of another should only do so when wearing breathing apparatus and whilst part of a controlled, monitored and co-coordinated rescue attempt.

6. CARGO WORK – HOLDS, HATCHES AND TANKS

The incident

A crew member was seriously injured when falling from the top of a hatch coaming to the main deck. The seafarer suffered head and brain injuries.

What happened?

After hose testing the cargo hatches on this five hold, nine hatch, bulk carrier, a failure of the sealing rubber on one of the forward hatch covers was identified. Replacement of the sealing rubber was given priority over other jobs and work commenced immediately. The seafarer was instructed by the chief officer who established the work area was oil free and presented no slipping risk. The seafarer was then left to work alone. He slipped backwards off the coaming top, which was approximately 300mm wide, falling some 2.5m to the main deck.

What went wrong?

The replacement of the hatch sealing rubber was considered to be a priority job by the chief officer. Thus the vessel's usually good work planning procedures were circumvented, the job was not correctly planned and all of the potential risks were not identified.

The job required suitable staging to be rigged with guard rails fitted. The seaman was not wearing a hard hat with chin strap, nor did he wear a safety harness.

When working aloft or where a fall of 2m or more is possible a safety harness should be worn. The seafarer was also left to work on his own when a stand-by man should have been appointed.

What can we learn from this incident?

Even when external pressures are present, safe practices, procedures and the correct use of personal protective equipment MUST ALWAYS be employed. If unplanned work is to be undertaken, an unscheduled work plan must be compiled and signed by the job supervisor and another senior officer. These persons should only sign permits when they are fully satisfied the job is well planned, correct safety equipment will be used and the personnel involved are made aware of all safety aspects.

CHAPTER 19

A SAFE COURSE AHEAD

In a loss prevention guide of this type it is not possible to cover every scenario individually. Rather the intention is to highlight those areas which regularly have a major influence in accidents and injuries.

The message from this guide is that, with the correct use of personal protective equipment, with good work planning and safety management and the adoption of safe work practices, accidents will be greatly reduced.

We must develop the Safety Ethos. This is not the adoption of a few safe practices; rather it is the wholesale review of safety policy and thinking. It is not something that will come overnight but requires initiation and support from the most senior personnel in the company.

Owners must realise that, although some practices have been carried out for years in a particular way, all procedures should be subject to continuous review and assessment. Where necessary, procedures should be changed to make them safer.

If a job is ever considered in any way to be unsafe, then it should be suspended until there is no doubt as to the safety of all personnel involved.

If the Safety Ethos is not fully developed, then safety will always be considered by some to be too expensive, inappropriate or unnecessary. Incorrect procedures will be adopted and it is the sea staff who will suffer injuries or worse be killed.

Any one injury is too expensive – certainly when the cost is human suffering.

We must continually remind seagoing personnel of the potential hazards and risks they encounter during their every day working. A useful means of reminding people of potential hazards and good practice is by using clear, unambiguous safety signs. Such signs and posters can be used to remind personnel when and where to wear certain protective equipment.

Safety drills and exercises enable personnel to become familiar with equipment on board ship and how to use it. When everyone is in tune with safety they automatically consider the safety aspects of the task in hand. Personnel remind each other, offer safety advice and only attempt duties they can complete safely.

Much of what this guide says is common sense or good seagoing practice, yet the author and the Association have seen enough accidents and personal injuries to know things go wrong far too often.

If you adopt the ideas offered in the guide and use the personal protective equipment provided you will hopefully avoid injury.

Keep a look out for yourself and others. The actions of others may cause you, themselves, or both, a serious injury.

At the end of the day, it is down to YOU!

Safe sailing.

INDEX

INDEX

INDEX